Assembly Language Essentials

A Guide to Powerful Programming for Embedded Systems

Assembly Language Essentials

A Guide to Powerful Programming for Embedded Systems

Larry Cicchinelli

Circuit Cellar, Inc.
www.circuitcellar.com

Assembly Language Essentials: A Guide to Powerful Programming for Embedded Systems

Published by
Circuit Cellar Inc.
4 Park Street
Vernon, CT 06066 USA

Notices

Knowledge and best practice in this field are constantly changing. As new research and experience broaden our understanding, changes in research methods, professional practices, or technologies may become necessary.

Practitioners and researchers must always rely on their own experience and knowledge in evaluating and using any information, methods, parts, electronics, designs, code, or experiments described herein. In using such information or methods they should be mindful of their own safety and the safety of others, including parties for whom they have a professional responsibility.

To the fullest extent of the law, neither the Publisher nor the authors, contributors, or editors, assume any liability for any injury and/or damage to persons or property as a matter of products liability, negligence or otherwise, or from any use or operation of any methods, products, instructions, or ideas contained in the material herein.

Library of Congress Control Number: 2011923558

ISBN 978-0-9630133-2-3

Prepress production: Eric A.J. Bogers
Cover Design: Helfrich Design
Printed by Wilco

109034-UK

Table of Contents

1
Terms and Definitions

Introduction

There seems to be a lack of general Assembly Language books available today. You can find information on the Internet for specific processors, but not much for learning how to program in Assembly Language in general terms. It is my hope that this book will at least partially fill this vacuum. The goal of this book is to get the reader to the point where he/she is reasonably familiar with the concepts of Assembly Language programming – not to make him/her an expert. Expertise only comes with practice, and becoming an expert in Assembly Language takes quite a bit of work.

Although my formal schooling was in Electrical Engineering, I have been programming in Assembly Language for most of my professional career, starting with the Hewlett Packard 2100 series, the 8008, 8080, 6800, 6805, 6811, PDP8™, PDP11™, VAX™, PIC™ and most recently the Rabbit™ series. Each has taught me more about Assembly Language programming, and thus I've become a better programmer. Each processor has advantages and disadvantages. The instruction sets have varied from fairly simple to quite complex.

The selection of a programming language should be based on the application's requirements. Typically, engineers choose Assembly language for a project when speed is a primary concern. Another valid reason is program size. Even though compilers are getting better at code generation, there are still applications for which hand coding yields a more efficient program. In today's embedded systems, there is usually a combination of both Assembly Language and a higher-level language.

Development time should also be a consideration. Any given task will probably take longer to develop in Assembly Language than in a higher-level language. If you project is time-constrained, you should consider using a higher language for the bulk of the program and Assembly Language only where absolutely necessary. If you are more constrained by program size, then Assembly Language may be a necessity.

The primary goal of this book is to teach Assembly Language and not to focus on a specific processor. With that goal in mind, I present a fictional processor with its own hardware and instruction set. Subsequent chapters cover various features and details of the processor used in this book. A number of references in this chapter and the next refer to features of "this processor."

Just another thought before you proceed – Assembly Language is probably not a good choice as a first programming language to learn. It is as close to the hardware of the processor as you can get. A good Assembly Language programmer will likely have a reasonably good understanding of hardware. If you have no previous programming experience, I highly recommend that you review a language such as C or BASIC in order to get an understanding of programming fundamentals.

Abbreviations

A number of abbreviations are typically used to describe features of processors and programming. The following abbreviations are used throughout this book. Learn them now if you don't already know them:

ALU	Arithmetic Logic Unit
CPU	Central Processing Unit
IPL	Interrupt Priority Level
ISR	Interrupt Service Routine
LSB	Least Significant Bit
MMU	Memory Management Unit
MSB	Most Significant Bit
PC	Program Counter
PSR	Processor Status Register
RAM	Random Access Memory
ROM	Read Only Memory
SP	Stack Pointer

CPU Architecture

There are many topics that can be addressed when discussing processors and programming them. In this section I describe some major CPU architecture features.

The starting point for learning how to program any processor in Assembly Language is its CPU architecture. The term CPU is often used to refer to the entire processor, but here I will use a more narrow definition which refers to the processor "core," where all of the high-speed logic is contained such as: the logic for the PC, instruction decode and execution, the ALU, etc. The ALU contains the logic for all of the arithmetic and logical operations.

There are several ways of describing general processor architecture. The following is a list of processor characteristics, some of which are comparisons. Most, if not all, of the following terms can be found on the Internet and with significantly more detail. The definitions are in alphabetical order just to make them easier to find. Attempting to put them in order of importance would be extremely difficult!

- Address Modes

Describe where the data values of an instruction are located. The PDP11 and VAX computers are examples of computers which use addressing modes extensively. With some other processors, such as the 8080, this mechanism is not quite as evident. Addressing Modes will be discussed in greater detail in a later chapter of this book; however, here are two examples:

  - Register – the data value is in the register

  - Register Indirect – the register contains the address of the data

- Atomic

  - The characteristic of a multi-byte value to be handled as a single entity

  - The feature that allows two instructions to execute without allowing interrupts to be acknowledged between them.

This can be explained better by example. Consider the case of updating a long integer (4 bytes) using an instruction set that does not have any 4 byte registers. In general, the update will take multiple instructions which means that an ISR accessing that value could access it during the update. This would result in a partially updated value being used by the ISR. Some processors have special instructions which do not allow interrupts to occur until after executing the following instruction. This feature would make the multi-instruction update occur as an atomic operation.

- Condition Codes

These are a set of bits which are used to determine several pieces of information about the results of the instruction just executed. (The instructions in some processors do not always affect the condition codes so their state is maintained through the execution of more than one instruction.) For instance: is the result zero or not, is the result positive or negative, are two values equal, etc.

For such a small architectural feature these bits have a huge affect on the program – they are the primary, if not the only, mechanism for making decisions. The condition code bits are often stored in the Processor Status Register. They are usually referenced in branch instructions which are a set of conditional jump instructions that test the state of one or more condition codes and execute the jump if the condition specified by the branch is met.

- DMA

Direct Memory Access is a mechanism that allows memory operations to occur independent of the CPU. It allows the processor to transfer data between memory and any of the following:

- Memory
- Internal I/O devices
- External I/O devices (see External I/O in I/O Devices)

Some implementations of DMA allow the transfer to occur while the CPU is executing at full speed, others suspend CPU operations because the DMA operations take over the buses. Quite a few parameters need to be set up in order for a DMA transfer to occur. Here is a partial list:

- Starting address of the data source
- Starting address of the data destination
- Number of bytes to transfer
- Flags indicating the devices (memory, IO) for the source and destination
- Priority

- Flash Memory

Flash memories are the primary program storage device used today in embedded systems. They are non-volatile, meaning that they maintain their content when power is removed, and are relatively easy to program. There are two types:

- Parallel

A program can be executed out of parallel flash. Most commercially available parallel flash devices today have an access time of at least 45ns. This will limit the maximum speed at which the processor can access the device to about 22MHz. Some systems will store the program in the flash but then copy it to a faster RAM for execution.

Serial

A program cannot be executed from serial flash. A system using serial flash for its program must copy it to a RAM for execution. It may take a little longer for the program to start due to the copying process but this method is quite cost effective and the additional start-up time is usually negligible.

Both parallel and serial flash devices can also be used as mass memories. Multi-gigabyte serial flashes are quite common now.

Harvard vs. von Neumann

Harvard processors have separate memories and buses for program and data. PIC processors are a good example.

Von Neumann processors use the same memory space for both program and data. The common PC today is a good example.

Most embedded systems today, although they use separate memory devices for program vs. data, are von Newmann architecture because they use the same address and data buses for accessing the memories.

I/O

An abbreviation for Input/Output. This term is used to refer to the "peripheral" devices which are built-in to the microprocessor or added externally. All I/O devices have registers which allow the programmer to configure and access them. Some examples are:

Parallel Ports

Serial Ports

Timers

Interrupt

Interrupts are a mechanism for "interrupting" the normal flow of the program. The events causing the interrupts can just as easily be from sources external to the CPU as well as internal to the processor. Many features of a processor can cause an interrupt, such as timers and communications devices. The source can also be from a signal generated external to the processor such as a switch closure.

Many processors have what are sometimes called Software Interrupts. These occur via a special set of instructions which are usually as short as the instruction set will allow. They are a method of essentially executing a short subroutine call. If the instruction set allows, some of the bits can be used to customize the instruction by allowing the programmer to specify their value which can then be decoded by the interrupt handler. When an interrupt occurs the processor will push the PC onto the stack and, in some systems, the PSR as well. It will then usually copy the contents of the appropriate Interrupt Vector into the Program Counter. Most processors will also set a new IPL based on data programmed into a register of the interrupting device.

Exiting from the Interrupt Service Routine usually involves executing a Return from Interrupt instruction which restores the PC (and the PSR if necessary). It is the responsibility of the programmer to ensure that all registers used during the ISR are restored to their pre-interrupt condition.One important feature of interrupts is that the processor will only acknowledge an interrupt between instruction executions. Another way of stating this is that an instruction cannot be interrupted during its execution. There are exceptions to this which will be noted in those instructions which are the exceptions.

Interrupt Vector

An Interrupt Vector is simply a pointer. It is a location in memory that contains the address of the routine to execute when the interrupt occurs – the Interrupt Service Routine or ISR. Most processors have a dedicated block of memory where all the interrupt vectors are stored.

Some processors also require that additional values be stored at the vector location. For instance, the PDP11 and VAX computers also store the interrupt priority as the second value for each vector entry.

Least Significant Bit

The LSB is the right-most bit in a sequence of bits. The bit number of the LSB is always 0[1]. See Most Significant Bit. This term should not be confused with Least Significant Byte. This book will always use the term LSB when referring to the Least Significant Bit.

Least Significant Byte

The LSByte is the right-most byte of a multi-byte value. The byte number of the LSByte is always 0. See Most Significant Byte.

This term should not be confused with Least Significant Bit. The LSB is always in the LSByte. This book will always use the term LSByte when referring to the Least Significant Byte.

1 I am not aware of any processors today that are different; however, I did work with one from PR1ME years ago that defined bit 1 as the MSB. In doing some research on this I found that some Honeywell computers also defined bit 1 as the MSB.

Little Endian vs. Big Endian

Describes where the Least Significant Byte of a value is stored

Little Endian means that for a multi-byte data value, the *least* significant byte (and bit) is located at the lowest address. Most microprocessors today are of this type.

Big Endian means that the *most* significant byte is located at the lowest address.

This can be a problem if you are transferring data between processors that are different in the way they store data values. You may need to do some byte re-ordering in one of the processors.

Load and Store

This refers to a property of the instruction set which defines that all operations, except LOAD and STORE, occur within registers. Basically, no address modes are allowed except for the LOAD and STORE instructions.

Memory Management Unit

One feature of the MMU is to allow the processor to access memory beyond the PC addressable range. Most systems do this by extending the PC based on decoding some number of upper PC bits. The PDP11 uses the upper 3 bits of the PC to select from among eight Page Address Registers which contain additional address bits that are combined with the original lower 13 of the PC. One way of using this system is to set Page Address Register zero to a value of 0. Doing this keeps page 0 always available.

Another method of Memory Management uses registers to define the boundaries between several blocks of memory within the PC addressable space. These blocks then have dedicated registers which define their physical addresses. This system is used by the Z180 and its derivatives. Another feature that Memory Management can provide is memory protection services. Special registers can be used to set ranges of memory defining them as being read-only. If a multitasking operating system is implemented, there could be registers that define the allowable memory for each task. These registers would be managed by the Task manager within the Operating System.

Memory Mapped I/O vs. Non-Memory Mapped I/O

Memory Mapped I/O implements the I/O registers in the same address space as the data. There is a dedicated range of addresses assigned to these registers. This method has the advantage of allowing the I/O registers to use the same instructions as are used to access the data.

Non-Memory Mapped I/O has the I/O registers in their own address space. This means that there must be special instructions, or an instruction prefix, used to access the registers. This method has the advantage of possibly having shorter instructions required to access the I/O registers.

Most Significant Bit

The MSB is the left-most bit in a sequence of bits. The bit number of the MSB is always one less than the total number of bits in the value. For instance: the MSB of a 32 bit value is bit 31. See Least Significant Bit. This term should not be confused with Most Significant Byte. This book will always use the term MSB when referring to the Most Significant Bit.

Most Significant Byte

The MSByte is the left-most byte of a multi-byte value. The byte number of the MSByte is always one less than the total number of bytes in the value. For instance: the MSByte of a 4 byte value is byte 3. See Least Significant Byte.

This term should not be confused with Most Significant Bit. The MSB is always in the MSByte. This book will always use the term MSByte when referring to the Most Significant Byte.

Number Format

Describes how numeric values are represented.

2's-Complement

This is probably the most common format used by computers today for integers. I am not aware of any modern processor which uses a different format for integer numeric values. In 2's-Complement arithmetic you can form the negative of a number by first inverting all the bits and then adding one.

For example: a +1 as a byte value in binary is 00000001. Inverting the bits yields 1111110 and then adding 1 yields 11111111. Taking the two values and adding them using binary arithmetic yields 0000000 (with a carry) which you would expect.

1's-Complement.

This representation simply inverts all the bits to form the negative. For example: a +1 as a byte value is 00000001, the same as 2's-complement. However, a negative 1 is 11111110. Using a simple binary adder on these two values yields 11111111. Obviously, something more complex than a simple binary adder is required.

Sign-Magnitude.

This representation simply uses the most significant bit as the sign bit while the remaining bits are the magnitude. A + 1 is still 00000001 while a – 1 is 1000001. An interesting side effect of this form is that you can have plus and minus zero! Floating point values use this format.

Binary Coded Decimal (BCD)

Some of the earliest computers were not binary! They actually used decimal arithmetic where each digit is represented with 4 bits. These also used a sign-magnitude representation to differentiate between positive and negative values. Here, a separate "bit" is used for the sign. An example of this format for the value 53 is: 0101 0011. Note that this format can be used to directly drive a seven segment display decoder.

Some of the early microprocessors, even though binary, had some instructions to handle this format. The 8080, which has a DAA instruction (Decimal Adjust after Addition), is an example. This instruction would be used after adding two bytes, both containing BCD encoded values, to modify the result in the A register so that sums up to 99 would be correctly represented in BCD.

Floating Point

Floating point refers to numeric values which have a decimal point in contrast to integers. There is a standard format for floating point values in binary computers. The following is for single precision (32 bits):

Sign bit
8 bits for the exponent
23 bit mantissa

For more information you should look up the IEEE 754-2008 standard.

There are values that cannot be represented exactly in floating point. Also, depending on the operations involved, due to rounding "errors" you may not get the exact value you expect. Because of these factors, it is not a good idea to test for equality when comparing floating point values.

Not all processors have floating point hardware. If not, they have to use software to handle the operations or have an external floating point processor.

An important feature to note is that with 23 bits of resolution you will get only 6 or 7 digits of resolution depending on the value.

Number of Bits

One of the most significant features used to characterize a processor is its "number of bits." This value usually refers to the width of the internal data bus. For instance, a 16 bit processor has a 16 bit wide internal data bus which is accessed by the CPU – including the ALU.

The width of this bus is one of two main contributors (the other is the register size) to how efficiently the processor can handle data. An n-bit processor will usually use n-bit memories. A processor using memories which are "wider" than n bits (usually double) will have to feed each set of n bits separately to the CPU for processing. Using memories which are "narrower" will require it to execute more memory accesses for a given operation.

This feature is sometimes used as a basis for either accepting or rejecting a processor for a particular application. This is, I believe, a misuse of the feature. A processor should be selected or rejected on whether or not it can do the job and certainly the data bus width can be a contributor but should probably not be the determining factor.

Operating Modes

This is a feature of some processors that allows specific features of the processor to be available to certain tasks. This can be very important in a multi-tasking environment. Those processors with this feature will have two or more modes available such as:

- System
- User

System mode controls the entire processor operation. It is the job of the System task to allocate resources to the various User tasks. It will even control when and if a User mode task executes. See Memory Management Unit for information on how System mode can affect memory utilization.

User mode is more restricted. It can only access memory and I/O devices which the System task has allowed it to access.

Orthogonal Instruction Set

The characteristic of an instruction set which allows the registers to be used interchangeably.

Basically, this means that most instructions can use any register. Again, the VAX and PDP11 are good examples. The 8080 and its derivatives do not have Orthogonal Instruction Sets. Another feature that is characteristic of an Orthogonal Instruction Set is that all arithmetic and logical instructions modify the condition codes uniformly.

In general, an Orthogonal Instruction Set requires more bytes per instruction than one that is not. For instance, the 8080 has quite a few single byte instructions. This would be impossible for a processor with an Orthogonal Instruction Set. It was extremely important for early microprocessors to have compact instruction sets in order to keep program size to a minimum.

This is a largely unnecessary restriction given today's technology. One advantage of an Orthogonal Instruction Set is that you can do more with a single instruction. In general, this leads to faster program development since fewer instructions are necessary to accomplish a given task.

Physical vs. Logical Memory

Physical Memory refers to the actual memory devices which are part of your system. This includes any memory that is internal to the processor as well as external memory devices. The physical memory of a system does not change during program execution.

Logical Memory refers to the memory which the PC can access at any given time. Logical memory of a system using memory management is constantly changing during program execution and is limited by the size of the PC. A 16 bit PC has a logical memory space of 65536 memory units, usually bytes.

Position Independent

The property of a block of assembled code that allows it to execute independent of its location in memory. This feature is completely dependent on the instruction set of the processor.

Processor Status Register

This register contains several pieces of information about the processor status. The amount of information in the PSR is largely determined by the size of the register. Most processors will have all or some of the following:

- Condition Code bits
- Current Register Set Number
- Interrupt Level
- Operating Mode

Program Counter

The PC is a high speed register that is used to address the memory devices containing the instructions to be executed. There is dedicated logic in the CPU which not only increments the PC as it proceeds through the stream of instructions, but can also modify the PC based on decisions and other calculations made by those instructions.

One very important feature of the PC is that as each part of an instruction is read from memory the PC is incremented by some value. In this processor, that value is two. One reason this is important is because of what happens when an interrupt occurs – the current value of the PC is pushed onto the stack. The "current value of the PC" will be the address of the next instruction so that when the "return from interrupt" instruction is executed, the processor will retrieve from the stack the address of the next instruction to be executed.

The size, in bits, of the PC determines the amount of memory that is directly addressable by the processor. For instance, a 16 bit PC can directly access 65,536 units. For most, if not all, processors today those units are bytes; however, they do not have to be. It is quite possible for those units to be words or even longwords (4 bytes). Again, some PIC versions are good examples of processors that use units other than bytes for its program space – their units are 12 bits. However, they do use bytes for data.

Many processors today use Memory Management techniques to extend their addressable memory into the many megabyte range (Physical Memory). This technique accesses program memory beyond the PC range (Logical Memory) by "mapping" the additional memory into the PC addressable space which makes the mapped memory look like it is within the addressable space. In many processors the size of the PC not only limits the size of the program but also the amount of data memory that can be accessed. This is because the mechanism for accessing data is often the same as that used for accessing the program. However, this need not be the case.

There are processors today which have general registers with more bits than the PC. They can have instructions that allow the contents of these registers to be used to drive the address bus for data access.

RAM and ROM

These are terms used to refer to the main types of memories used in programming a microprocessor.

RAM is an abbreviation for Random Access Memory. Initially, the term was used in contrast to sequentially accessed memory such as disk drives. In today's systems it refers to memory that can be modified by the program. RAM will contain all of the variables of the program and the stack.

ROM is an abbreviation for Read Only Memory; however, most ROM devices are just as much random access as RAM. In most embedded systems the program is stored in a ROM of some type. In many systems parallel flash memory is used and is handled as if it is ROM.

Registers

You really need to understand the registers and how the instruction set uses them if you are going to be successful with any Assembly Language programming. The registers are basically high speed memories built into the CPU. They are used by most instructions to perform the arithmetic and logical operations required to execute the program. The size of the registers is a major contributor to how efficiently the processor can handle data values (the other is the "number of bits"). For instance, a processor with only 8 bit registers will have to perform multiple instructions to handle 16 bit (and larger) arithmetic.

RISC vs. CISC

RISC stands for Reduced Instruction Set Computer. Quite a few computers today may say they are RISC but what they really mean is that a single clock cycle is required for most, if not all, instructions. The PIC processors are a good example of a truly RISC processor.

CISC stands for Complex Instruction Set Computer. Most microprocessors today are of this type. Usually they require multiple clock cycles to execute each instruction.

Signed vs Unsigned

Signed values can be either positive or negative. The range of signed integers (and unsigned as well) is completely dependent on the number of bits being used. As an example, an eight bit signed value using two's complement format has a range of –128 to +127. The range for 16 bit integers is –32768 to +32767. The formula for the range is:

maximum positive value is $2^{(N-1)} - 1$
maximum negative value is $-1 * 2^{(N-1)}$

Since 0 is considered positive, there are the same number of positive and negative values.

Unsigned values are always positive. There are several instances where unsigned values should be used. Some of them are:

addresses
counters
array indices

The maximum value for an unsigned integer is: $2^N - 1$.

In many cases it does not matter whether signed or unsigned values are used. However, there are many where it can be quite important. If you are using a calculated value as an index into memory an unsigned value should be used. Using a signed value will usually lead to trouble. This is probably more important in high level languages but improper use of signed vs unsigned values can lead to problems that are hard to detect even in Assembly Language.

- Stack and Stack Pointer

  The stack is a special section of RAM that is utilized for:

  - Storing the return address when a function or subroutine call is executed
  - Storing the return address (and PSR) when an interrupt is recognized
  - Temporary storage of variables and registers
  - It is usually a Last-In-First-Out block of memory

There are several terms associated with accessing stack data:

- Push – the process of putting data onto the stack
- Pull (also sometimes called Pop) – the process of retrieving data from the stack
- Top of the Stack – the address of the last value pushed onto the stack
- Bottom of the Stack – the address to which the SP is initialized

Note: these last two definitions may seem backward since the Top of the Stack is at a lower address than the Bottom of the stack. The definitions arise from the way the stack is used – the stack builds down in memory and the operation of placing a value onto the top of a stack seems more reasonable than placing a value into the bottom.

The stack usually has a maximum amount of RAM allocated to it. Attempting to use the stack beyond this amount will cause problems such as writing on top of values stored below the stack or attempting to write to (or read) nonexistent memory. Some processors have special features for detecting stack overflow, attempting to push too much data on the stack, and stack underflow, attempting to pull too much data from the stack. The Stack Pointer is a CPU register which should contain the address within the stack of the next value available value to be pulled from the stack – the Top of the Stack. In some processors the SP contains the address of the next available stack location.

For many processors the operation of pushing a value onto the stack is:

- Subtract the data size from the current value of the SP
- Write the data value to the memory address contained in the SP

To pull a value from the stack:

- Read the data value, based on its size, from the address contained in the SP
- Add the size of the data value to the SP

These two operations are sometimes referred to as pre-decrement and post-increment respectively. As can be seen from these operations, as the number of values on the stack increases the memory address in the SP gets lower. Another way of saying this is that the stack builds down in memory. There are processors that utilize essentially the opposite method: post-decrement and pre-increment. The 6800 is one such processor.

It is extremely important that the SP be initialized as one of the first, if not the first, operations of a program and certainly before interrupts are enabled or any functions are called. In a pure Assembly Language program, the programmer must decide where in RAM the stack is going to reside, allocate the memory and set the SP to the "bottom" of the stack. If there are stack error detection mechanisms, they should all be initialized at the same time.

2
What is Assembly Language?

Assembly language is generally considered as the lowest level of programming languages[1]. Sometimes it is referred to as machine code; however, machine code is really the 1's and 0's that make up the binary values which the processor actually executes. For any given processor there is a 1:1 relationship[2] between assembly language and machine code – every assembly language statement has exactly one machine code equivalent and every machine code value has exactly one assembly language equivalent.

Assuming there is no operating system, when you program in Assembly Language you are in complete control of the processor and what it is doing. Your program has to do everything. You cannot simply add two numbers and print the result. You have to write the step-by-step instructions to get the numbers, add them and then display the sum. The following example gives you an idea of the details involved.

As an introduction to Assembly Language here is a very simple C program followed by an explanation of the assembly language statements the compiler generated:

```
main ()
{
    int         int_a;
    long        long_a;
    float       float_a;

    int_a = 1;
    long_a = 1;
    float_a = 1;                // the compiler automatically
```

1 The only possible exception would be that of microprogramming. Very simply put, microprogramming is a technique for implementing assembly language instructions using even lower level instructions. Each assembly language instruction consists of one or more micro-instructions. However, I am not aware of any current processors that use microprogramming. You can find several discussions on the Internet about microprogramming, but all the ones I found pre-date 1995.

2 In some very rare cases, one assembly language statement can have two machine code equivalents.

```
                                  // "promotes" the integer 1
                                  // to a floating point value

        float_a = 1 + int_a;      // the compiler automatically...
    }
```

The compiler used for this example is Dynamic C™, version 10.56, for a Rabbit™ 5000 processor. The compiler will first generate Assembly Language statements and then pass them to an Assembler. Below are the assembly language statements which were generated. Comments have been inserted that describe each statement as well as some explanatory notes.The compiler uses lower case letters for the registers – they have been changed to upper case to make them easier to read. First, a few comments about the statements that follow:

- The syntax of each statements is: instruction argument one, argument two.
  - Some instructions do not have argument two.
- The C source statements are on lines by themselves and are shown as comments.
  - Comments are indicated using a ';'
- The first text on each of the generated lines is the assembly language instruction
  - add — add the value of argument two to the value of argument one leaving the result in the location specified by argument one.
  - ld — copy the value of argument two to the location specified in argument one
  - lcall — call the function (or subroutine) indicated by the argument
  - clr — clear (put a value of 0 into) the contents of the argument
- The 16 bit registers are
  - SP — Stack Pointer
  - HL — The combined H and L registers (8 bits each), H is the MSByte
  - BC — The combined B and C registers (8 bits each), B is the MSByte
  - DE — The combined D and E registers (8 bits each), D is the MSByte

The only 32 bit register is BCDE – the combined B, C, D and E registers (8 bits each), B is the MSByte

"0x" is a prefix for hexadecimal values

```
    add     SP, -10                ; make room on the stack for the auto
                                   ; variables
```

Since these are all auto variables, they will be placed on the stack. The compiler is inserting code which allocates 10 bytes of stack space – int_a requires 2 bytes, long_a and float_a both require 4 bytes. The Rabbit instruction set does not have a subtract instruction that uses SP.

```
; int_a = 1;
    ld      HL, 0x0001             ; load an integer value of 1 into the
                                   ; HL register (16 bits)
    ld      (SP + 0x08), HL        ; store the contents of HL into
                                   ; the auto variable location
                                   ; for int_a
```

This processor does not have an instruction that loads a constant directly to a memory location.

```
; long_a = 1;
    ld      BCDE, 1                ; load an integer value of 1 into the
                                   ; BCDE register (32 bits)
    ld      (SP + 0x04), BCDE      ; store the contents of BCDE
                                   ; into the auto variable
                                   ; location for long_a

; float_a = 1;
    ld      BCDE, 0                ; load a value of 0 into the BCDE
                                   ; register (32 bits)
    ld      BC, 0x3F80             ; load the most significant 16 bits of
                                   ; a floating point 1.0 into register
                                   ; BC
    ld      (SP + 0x00), BCDE      ; store the contents of BCDE
                                   ; into the auto variable
                                   ; location for float_a
```

The lower 2 bytes of a floating point value of 1.0 are 0. The compiler "knows" how to construct the needed binary pattern.

```
; float_a = 1 + int_a;
   ld      HL, (SP + 0x08)       ; load the contents of the auto
                                 ; variable int_a into register HL
   ld      DE, 0x0001            ; load an integer value of 1 into
                                 ; the DE register (16 bits)
   add     HL, DE                ; add the contents of DE to the
                                 ; contents of HL
```

The compiler recognizes the two values being added as integers. It also recognizes that the constant value (1) can be represented with 16 bits and is the same size as the variable so they can be added without having to convert either of them to a compatible data type.

```
   lcall   Hi_Bf                 ; convert the integer value in HL to
                                 ; floating point and store in BCDE
```

Since the values just added result in an integer value the compiler recognizes that the result must be converted to floating point. The compiler will include the function Hi_Bf in the code to do the conversion. From examining the statements we can conclude that the function wants the integer value in HL and returns the result in BCDE.

```
   clr     HL                    ; offset on the stack for the auto
                                 ; variable float_a
   add     HL, SP                ; add the contents of the stack
                                 ; pointer to HL to get the address of
                                 ; float_a
```

Obviously, simply copying SP to HL will accomplish the same thing or even better – loading BCDE directly to (SP). However, the code generator must handle the general case. I am not a compiler writer but I imagine that optimizing the code for this case might prove to be somewhat difficult.

```
   ld      (HL), BCDE            ; store the contents of BCDE into the
                                 ; auto variable location for float_a
```

As you can see from the generated code, programming in Assembly Language is quite different from higher level languages. You have to do everything yourself. Even the code shown above does not show all the code generated by the compiler (i.e., the code for the Hi_Bf function). Also, since the code above was generated for a C environment there is lots of other code that does not have anything to do directly with the C statements but that are used to set up the target processor, debugging, etc.

When programming in assembly language, the programmer must think of every detail involved in the process for the task at hand. The following outline shows exactly what this means. The task is to add two numbers and display the result.

- Get the first number
- Get the second number
- Add them
- Display them

The outline seems simple enough, but exactly how do you program each of the steps? It depends entirely on the processor: the instructions and hardware it supports. There are questions which need to be answered:

- What kind of numbers are they?
  - Integer
    - 16 bits
    - 32 bits
  - Floating point
    - Single precision
    - Double precision
- Are they both the same kind?
- Does the program have to support whatever numbers are entered?
- How does the program get the numbers?
  - Constants embedded in the program
  - Operator entry
- What protocol is used to communicate with the display

These questions need to be asked whatever the programming language, but in assembly language the implementation is quite a bit more difficult.

That implementation depends on a number of factors based on the processor:

- Does the processor have floating point hardware
- What size are the registers
- How many registers does it have
- Is it an orthogonal instruction set
- What kind of I/O devices does it have

A higher level language allows the programmer to ignore most, if not all, of these questions. For instance – if the processor does not support floating point hardware, there will be software functions available to handle the floating point operations (as in the above sample). If the processor has only eight and/or 16 bit registers, the compiler will have functions to handle the arithmetic operations that require more than eight or 16 bits.

Here is a more detailed outline that will probably suffice for a pure assembly language implementation. The assumption is that both values will be entered via a serial interfaced terminal and that the result will be displayed on that same terminal.

- Define whatever memory configuration values are necessary
- Allocate RAM for all variables – including terminal input
- Allocate ROM for and define all messages to be sent to the terminal
- Ask for the first value
    - This probably requires using a UART and the software driver necessary for accessing it
    - The driver needs to be written
- Get the value
    - Again – this requires a UART and the driver which will have to be written
- Determine the data type, convert and store the binary value accordingly
    - This is not as easy as it may sound:
        - Check for a leading '–' to see if it is negative
        - Check for a leading '+'
        - Is there a decimal point – making it floating point?
        - Does the program have to support 'E' format?
- Ask for the second value
- Get the value
- Determine the data type, convert and store the binary value accordingly
- Add the two values based on their data type

- Convert the sum to ASCII
- Display a message with the result

As you can see there is quite a bit of detail involved in writing an Assembly Language program. However, in most cases you will probably not be writing an entire program – you will be writing one or more functions in Assembly Language. As stated elsewhere in this book, one of the main reasons for writing in Assembly Language is execution speed. If your application is written in C, or any other high level language, and it requires any high speed processing you may need to consider writing some function(s) in Assembly Language. This is especially true for Interrupt Service Routines which should be executed as quickly as possible.

As is the case with most things, the only way to become proficient with Assembly Language is to use it. There are several exercises later in this book which can be used to get you started. Although this book is not about any specific processor, the skills acquired learning the Assembly Language for any processor can be used immediately with any other.

Basically you will need to learn the syntax of the new instructions, the register set and processor architecture. This is not as difficult as it may at first seem. There are certainly differences but usually once you have learned the Assembly Language for one processor, learning the details of another processor is relatively easy.

High Level Language Calling Conventions

In many cases your Assembly Language code will have to interface to a higher level language, sometimes abbreviated HLL. These interfaces will usually fall into one of two categories:

1. Stand-alone such as is found in an Interrupt Service Routine
2. Called from the HLL

There are a few examples of ISRs in Chapter 11 of this book. The main criteria you need to consider in an ISR, as far as the HLL is concerned, is the preservation of registers. When the interrupt occurs, your ISR code has no idea of how the HLL is using the processors registers so it is up to the ISR to both save and restore any registers it uses which may also be in use by the calling function. All of this is discussed in more detail in Chapter 11.

When an Assembly language function is called from an HLL, it is up to the compiler, or interpreter, to define the calling convention. In general, the HLL will allow the called function to use all available registers. However, there are strict rules for passing parameters such as:

- The first argument may be put into a specific register. The register that is used may be dependent on the size of the argument and whether or not the argument is a pointer.

- All arguments, including the first, are usually pushed onto the stack. In most cases the last argument is the first one pushed on the stack. This makes the first argument the last one pushed on the stack.

- Some systems may put the number of arguments as the last value pushed. This will only be required if the number of arguments is variable.

- It is up to the called function to "know" the data type, size and stack offset for each argument.

- Global values can usually be accessed directly by referencing their names.

- Local values, usually stored on the stack, will need to be accessed using a compiler/interpreter defined method.

  See chapter 6 for definitions of Global and Local.

- Keep in mind that the last item pushed onto the stack is the return address.

- A return value will usually be put into a specific register.

You need to read the compiler/interpreter documentation and thoroughly understand the conventions it uses for calling Assembly Language functions. Debugging Assembly Language can be difficult but it will be considerably more so if these rules are not strictly followed. Here are two possibilities for errors:

1 Using a register which must be preserved but you do not. Your function may execute just fine but the program will eventually crash.

2 Using parameters off the stack with the incorrect size or retrieving them with an incorrect stack offset will cause your function to execute incorrectly.

3
Address Modes

Every processor uses address modes of some kind. This is true even of processors that do not have an Orthogonal Instruction Set. Understanding the address modes is one of the keys to successful Assembly Language programming. This chapter will discuss address modes in general – including some which are not used in this processor. The following discussions are generalities and details may be different for some processors.

Here is a list of some address modes:

Immediate	the argument is the operand
Register	the content of the register is the operand
Register indirect	the register contains the address (sometimes called a pointer) of the operand
Register offset	the register value plus a constant is the address of the operand
Address	the argument is the address of the operand
Address indirect	the argument is the address of the address of the operand
Auto increment and decrement	an extension of register indirect where the register value is incremented or decremented by the data size either before or after retrieving the operand
PC relative	the argument is an offset value to the operand

More complete definitions (and examples) are found later in this chapter.

The terms argument and operand may be confusing. This book uses the term operand to refer to a data value. The term argument is essentially a place holder which will be either an operand or lead to an operand. An example may help:

```
ADD    #15, (R0)        ; add the value 15 to the contents of
                        ; the address contained in R0
```

Both the "#15" and "(R0)" are arguments. The "#15" is also an operand since it is a value. The "(R0)" is not an operand since R0 is not a data value – it contains an address. The content of that address is the operand.

Before getting into the address modes themselves, we need to discuss instruction formats. Here is a brief explanation of some of the notation used in the samples:

- For an instruction that has a suffix of a period and single digit, the digit is the number of bytes in the operand(s). Other assemblers may use different syntax. Here are two examples that do exactly the same thing:

  - INC.2 – increment a 2 byte value. This is the syntax used in this book.

  - INCW – increment a word value.

- A value with a prefix of "0x" indicates a hexadecimal number.

- The registers will be shown as: R0, R1,...

- The construction (Rn) means to use the contents of Register n as an address.

- The character "@" means that the result of an expression is an address.

- The character "#" indicates that the argument is the operand.

- The instructions and register names are not case sensitive.

- ??? indicates that the value is not relevant and could be anything.

- All numeric values, including those that represent addresses, can be anything, but a value is indicated just for purposes of the example.

- IMPORTANT: Assembler syntax and rules are very much implementation dependent. There is no guarantee that the syntax used in one assembler is going to be the same in another – even for the same processor!

Another note on a subject that may be obvious to many but, if you are quite new to programming...

There is a major difference between the address of a value and the value itself. Here is a quick example using the copy instruction:

```
COPY    #location1, R0        ; copy the address of location1
                              ; into R0

COPY    location1, R0         ; copy the contents of location1
                              ; into R0
```

Most processors will have at least the following types of instructions:

- No argument or operand

There are very few of these.

Example: `RTS` ; return from subroutine

- Single argument or operand

Here are a few of the classes of single argument instructions

- Integer arithmetic

Example: `INC R0` ; add 1 to the contents of R0

- Logical

Example: `RL R0` ; rotate R0 1 bit to the left

- Program Counter

Example: `JMP Location_1` ; jump to address Location_1

- Double argument or operand

Most of these will be arithmetic instructions. In most cases the argument one operand is not modified and the argument two operand receives the result of the operation. For this processor, as demonstrated in the following example, the argument two operand is also the destination where the result will be placed.

Example:

```
ADD    R0,R1          ; add the contents of R0 to the
                      ; contents of R1
```

IMPORTANT: The operand order is not fixed by the processor – it is defined by the assembler. This instruction could just as easily be written as follows, dependent on the assembler requirements:

Example:
```
ADD   R1,R0          ; add the contents of R0 to the
                     ; contents of R1
```

The assembler for this processor uses the first form.

Triple argument or operand (usually only found in processors which are 32 bits or greater)

Similar to double operand except that the third operand receives the result of the operation. Neither of the other two operands is modified.

Example:
```
ADD   R0, R1, R2     ; add the contents of R0 and the
                     ;contents of R1. Place the result
                     ; in R2
```

Instruction Execution Time

Correctly assessing instruction execution time can be an important part of your Assembly Language programming experience. If you are going to be writing ISRs, then you will be very interested in instruction timing. The timing values shown in the following discussions are described in terms of clock cycles, so that they are independent of the actual CPU clock speed. Most, if not all, manuals that describe an instruction set will define execution times in terms of CPU clock cycles.

This was not always the case. Earlier processors, mini-computers and mainframes, had fixed clock speeds. The timing of the instructions was fixed and usually defined in terms using microseconds.

The timing values in this book make an assumption which may not be true for all microprocessor systems – a single clock cycle is required to access a byte or word independent of its alignment. The alignment of a word (a 2 byte value) is an indication of whether it begins on an odd address or an even address. In some systems accessing a word value which begins on an odd address takes an additional cycle.

Another feature of some memories is that they take additional time to access the first location in a “page” of the memory device. Additional accesses to the same page can be made without that additional time.

Usually that additional time is 1 clock cycle, but it could be something more complex. The page size can vary among devices but 16 bytes seems to be common today.

This table shows the number of clocks required to access different numbers of bytes in the instructions:

1 byte = 1 additional clock
2 bytes = 1 additional clock
4 bytes = 2 additional clocks
8 bytes = 4 additional clocks

The number of clocks is the same for both reading and writing. An argument that has a memory location as a destination will usually require a read-modify-write (read from memory, modify the value, write it back) operation and thus require double the number of clocks indicated.

Some instructions will require additional clocks in order to perform the operation.

Just as a reminder – these times are for this processor and are due to the data bus being 16 bits. Having additional clocks is typical of most processors but the details can vary.

Instruction Length

The number of bytes an instruction requires is determined by several factors:

The basic architecture of the processor
The number of operands
The size of the operands – usually dependent on the Address Modes being used

As has already been mentioned, many processors allow single byte instructions. These processors probably do not have an Orthogonal Instruction Set. This processor does and its instructions are always an even number of bytes. The base instruction, often referred to as the opcode, is always 2 bytes.

The following discussion on Address Modes will expand on the instruction size for each mode.

Address Modes

Here are a few features of this processor that may help understand the following discussions:

Unless explicitly indicated, all values are decimal.
Addresses are 32 bits
The registers in this processor are 64 bits (8 bytes).
Only the lowest n bytes, as specified by the operation, of the registers are affected by the instructions

Register – The operand is the value in the register. No additional clocks or bytes are required.

This is one of the easier modes to understand. This first example below has 2 arguments both of which are register mode: the contents of R0 are copied to R1. The original content of R1 is overwritten.

Most assemblers allow you to simply use the register name in the syntax of the statements. Usually no additional clock cycles are required for the argument(s).

Example:

```
COPY.2   R0, R1   ; copy the content of R0 to R1 – only the
                  ;lower 2 bytes are used/affected – as
                  ; indicated by the .2 suffix
```

Fig. 3.1

	R0	R1
Before	0xABCD1234	???
After	0xABCD1234	???1234

Total execution time is 1 clock:

1 = read the basic instruction

Since the destination is register mode, no additional clocks are required to write the result.

Total memory usage is 2 bytes:

2 bytes for the COPY instruction
No additional bytes for the arguments since they are both register mode – the register numbers are contained in the opcode.

These two examples show the effect of the data size on the result:

```
INC.2    R0       ; add 1 to the 2 byte value in R0 – only the
                  ; lower 2 bytes are affected
```

Fig 3.2

	R0
Before	0xABCDFFFF
After	0xABCD0000

```
INC.4     R0          ; add 1 to the 4 byte value in R0 – only the
                      ; lower 4 bytes are affected
```

Fig. 3.3

	R0
Before	0xABCDFFFF
After	0xABCE0000

Total execution time for both examples:

1 = read the basic instruction
1 = perform the INC instruction

Since the destination is register mode, no additional clocks are required to write the result.

Total memory usage:

2 bytes for the INC instruction
No additional bytes for the argument since it is register mode

Immediate – The value is in the instruction stream and follows the instruction opcode. The number of additional clocks and bytes are dependent on the operand size.

Immediate mode can usually be used only for one argument. Some assemblers allow you to specify a value with no special notation for an immediate value (example 1) but some do require special notation (example 2). Additional clock cycles are required to read the value into the CPU. The number of cycles will vary by processor but is usually 1 cycle per memory access.

Example:

```
COPY.1    5, R0       ; copy a single byte value of 5 to R0 – only
                      ; the lowest byte is affected
```

Fig. 3.4

	R0
Before	0x1234
After	0x1205

Total execution time is 2 clocks:

1 = read the basic instruction
1 = read argument one

Since the destination is register mode, no additional clocks are required to write the result.

Total memory usage is 4 bytes:

- 2 bytes for the COPY instruction
- 2 additional bytes for argument one since it is immediate mode, no bytes for argument two

Note: 2 bytes are required for argument one for this processor since all instructions must be an even number of bytes.

Example:

```
ADD.2     #0x1234, R0   ; add 0x1234 to the contents of R0 -
                        ; only the lower 2 bytes are
                        ; used/affected
```

Fig. 3.5

	R0
Before	0x????1205
After	0x????2439

Total execution time is 3 clocks:

- 1 = read the basic instruction
- 1 = read argument one
- 1 = perform the ADD instruction

Since the destination is register mode, no additional clocks are required to write the result.

Total memory usage is 4 bytes:

- 2 bytes for the COPY instruction
- 2 additional bytes for argument one since it is immediate mode, no bytes for argument two

Register Indirect – also known as **Register Deferred** – The operand is at the address specified in the register. Additional clocks are required for each Register Indirect mode but no additional bytes.

The number of additional clocks is dependent on the operand size. More clocks will be required to write the result if the destination mode is Indirect.

Example:

```
ADD.2    (R0), (R1)    ; add the value whose address is in R0
                       ; to the value whose address is in R1 -
                       ; only the lower 2 bytes are
                       ; used/affected
```

Fig. 3.6

	R0	R1	contents of 1234	contents of 5678
Before	00001234	00005678	0xABCD	0x12AB
After	00001234	00005678	0xABCD	0xBE78

Note: for this instruction, as well as others where the register content is an address, the register value is shown as a 32 bit value.

Total execution time is 5 clocks:

1 = read the basic instruction
1 = read operand from the address specified in R0
1 = read operand from the address specified in R1
1 = perform the ADD instruction
1 = write the result to the address specified in R1

Total memory usage is 2 bytes:

2 bytes for the ADD instruction
No additional bytes for the arguments since they are both register indirect mode

Example:

```
INC.4    (R0)    ; increment the value whose address is in R0
                 ; - only the lower 4 bytes are
                 ; used/affected. Note that it takes 2 clocks
                 ; to access a 4 byte value.
```

Fig. 3.7

	R0	contents of 1234
Before	00001234	0xABCD
After	00001234	0xABCE

Total execution time is 6 clocks:

1 = read the basic instruction
2 = read operand from the address specified in R0

1 = perform the INC instruction
2 = write the result to the address specified in R0

Total memory usage is 2 bytes:

2 bytes for the ADD instruction
No additional bytes for the argument since it is register indirect mode

Offset – The operand is at the address calculated by adding an offset value to the contents of the register. The offset value will be sign extended from 16 bits to 32 bits before adding it to the register content. Two additional bytes are required for each Offset mode argument.

Two additional clocks are required for each Offset mode argument:

1 = read in the offset value
1 = calculate the address
More clocks are required for accessing the operand(s) depending on the size

More clocks will be required to write the result if the destination mode is Offset but only those required to do the actual write since the address is already known.

Example:

```
ADD.2     234(R0), 3678(R1)     ; add the 2 byte values – only
                                ; the lower 2 bytes are
                                ; used/affected
```

Fig. 3.8

	R0	R1	contents of 1234	contents of 5678
Before	00001000	00002000	0xABCD	0x12AB
After	00001000	00002000	0xABCD	0xBE78

Operand one address = 234 + 1000 = 1234
Operand two address = 3678 + 2000 = 5678
0xABCD + 0x12AB = 0xBE78

Total execution time is 9 clocks:

1 = read the basic instruction
2 = read argument one offset and calculate operand one address
1 = read operand one value of 2 bytes
2 = read argument two offset and calculate operand two address
1 = read operand two value of 2 bytes

1 = perform the ADD instruction
1 = write the result to the operand two address

Total memory usage is 4 bytes:

2 bytes for the ADD instruction
2 bytes for each Offset mode argument

Example:

```
INC.2    234(R0)   ; increment the value whose address is
                   ; formed by adding 234 to the contents
                   ; of R0.
```

Fig. 3.9

	R0	contents of 1234
Before	1000	0xABCD
After	1000	0xABCE

Total execution time is 6 clocks:

1 = read the basic instruction
2 = read argument offset and calculate operand address
1 = read operand of 2 bytes
1 = perform the INC instruction
1 = write the result to the operand address

Total memory usage is 4 bytes:

2 bytes for the INC instruction
2 bytes for the offset value of the argument

Offset Indirect or **Offset Deferred**– The addition of the offset and the register content is the address of an address. Two additional bytes are required for each Offset Indirect mode argument. Four additional clocks are required for each Offset Indirect mode argument:

1 = read in the offset value
1 = add the offset to the register value to get the address of the address
2 = read the address of the operand (reminder: the address is 2 words)
Additional clocks are required for accessing the operand dependent on its size

More clocks will be required to write the result if the destination mode is Offset Indirect but only those required to do the actual write since the address is already known.

Example:

```
ADD.2     @234(R0), R1     ; add the 2 byte values
```

Fig. 3.10

	R0	R1	contents of 1234	contents of 5678
Before	1000	25	5678	75
After	1000	100	5678	75

Operand one address = @(234 + 1000) = @1234 = 5678

Total execution time is 7 clocks:

1 = read the basic instruction
2 = read argument one offset and calculate address of address
2 = read 4 byte address of operand
1 = read 2 byte operand
0 = read argument two operand of 2 bytes
1 = perform the ADD instruction
0 = write the result to argument two

Total memory usage is 4 bytes:

2 bytes for the ADD instruction
2 bytes for the offset value of argument one

Auto-Increment/Decrement – These modes are similar to Register Indirect but with an additional feature: the specified register is incremented (or decremented) by the size of the operand. One additional clock is required for each Auto Increment/Decrement mode to calculate the operand address and one to modify the register value.

Additional clocks are required for each Auto Increment/Decrement mode and is dependent on the operand size. More clocks will be required to write the result if the destination mode is Auto Increment/Decrement but only those required to do the actual write since the address is already known.

This mode is very handy for stepping through tables. Also, the increment/decrement operation can take place either before or after handling the operand. The four combinations can be summarized as: pre/post increment/decrement. The examples below use a "+" to indicate increment and a "–" to indicate decrement.

If the symbol precedes the register the operation is pre increment/decrement. If the symbol follows the register the operation is post increment/decrement. The value by which the register changes is determined by the operand size specified in the instruction.

Example:

```
ADD.2    (R0)+, -(R1)    ; both R0 and R1 contain addresses. R0
                         ; will be incremented by two after
                         ; retrieving the operand. R1 will be
                         ; decremented by two before retrieving
                         ; the operand and storing the result
```

Fig. 3.11

	R0	R1	contents of 1234	contents of 5676
Before	1234	5678	0xABCD	0x12AB
After	1236	5676	0xABCD	0xBE78

Operand one address = (R0) = 1234
Operand two address = (R1 - 2) = 5676

Total execution time is 7 clocks:

1 = read the basic instruction
0 = use content of R0 as an address
1 = read operand one
1 = add two to R0
1 = subtract two from R1
0 = use content of R1 as an address
1 = read operand two
1 = perform the ADD instruction
1 = write the result to operand two address

Total memory usage is 4 bytes:

2 bytes for the ADD instruction
No additional bytes for the arguments since they are both essentially register indirect mode

Just as an interesting note: processors which support using the Stack Pointer as a general register use these addressing modes to access the stack. For instance, the PDP11 uses the following for storing and retrieving values to and from the stack:

```
MOV     R0, -(SP)    ; push the contents of R0 onto the stack

MOV     (SP)+, R0    ; pull contents for R0 from the stack
```

After executing both of these instructions both R0 and the Stack Pointer will have the same content as before execution of the instructions.

Auto-Increment/Decrement Indirect – Same as Auto-Increment/Decrement except that the register contains the address of an address. Three additional clocks are required for each Auto-Increment/Decrement Indirect mode:

2 = retrieve the operand address
1 = update the register by four because it contains an address

Additional clocks are required for each Auto Increment/Decrement Indirect mode and is dependent on the operand size. More clocks will be required to write the result if the destination mode is Auto Increment/Decrement but only those required to do the actual write since the address is already known.

Example:

```
ADD.2    @(R0)+, R1
```

Fig. 3.12

	R0	R1	contents of 1234	contents of 5678
Before	1234	25	5678	75
After	1238	100	5678	75

Operand one address = @(R0) = @1234 = 5678

Total execution time is 6 clocks:

1 = read the basic instruction
0 = use content of R0 as address of address
2 = read 4 byte address
1 = update R0
1 = read 2 byte operand one
1 = perform the ADD instruction
0 = store value in R1

Total memory usage is 2 bytes:

2 bytes for the ADD instruction
No additional bytes for the arguments

Address Relative – Same as Offset except that it uses the Program Counter as the register. Additional clocks and bytes are required for each Address Relative argument.

Some processors allow you to access the PC as if it were one of the general purpose registers. This enables an assembler to easily generate code that is position independent. The PDP11 and VAX computers are good examples.

Consider the case of a function that has some local values which must be stored (or retrieved) in the same memory as the program. This could be the case for any von Neumann processor in which the program runs in RAM. With this type of addressing the function can be compiled so that it can be loaded anywhere in memory.

Example:

```
ADD.2    1996(PC), R0    ; the address of operand one is 3000
```

Fig. 3.13

	PC	R0	contents of 3000
Before	00001000	1234	4567
After	00001004	5801	4567

The contents of the PC are added to the offset value to create the address of the first operand. The contents of that address are then added to the existing contents of R0. The reason the offset value is 1996 instead of 2000 is that the PC is incremented with each memory fetch. The first memory fetch is for the instruction itself and the second is to get the offset value, so by the time the ALU can calculate the address of the operand the PC has been advanced by four.

In general, the programmer does not need to be concerned with this mechanism. The assembler "knows" how the PC operates and generates the correct value for the offset as long as the programmer uses a symbol to refer to the desired value.

Example:

```
ADD.2    Value, R0    ; add the contents of address Value to
                      ; the contents of R0
```

The Assembler is smart enough to recognize this as an Address Relative for argument one and handle it accordingly. It will calculate the needed offset and put the correct value into the instruction stream. An assembler that recognizes this mode will also have special symbols for Immediate and Address Absolute modes in order to differentiate among them.

Example:

```
JMPR     SomeAddress    ; jump to the location defined by the
                        ; label "SomeAddress"
```

The assembler recognizes the JMPR instruction as "jump relative." The value calculated by the assembler for part of the instruction is the *offset* between the next instruction (after the PC has been advanced) and the specified address. The number of bytes (or bits) required for the offset is dependent on the architecture of the processor. In this processor the offset is 20 bits, but four of those bits are stored in the opcode. Also, the assembler will generate an error message if the calculated offset to the address is too large.

Address Absolute – The argument is the address of the operand. Two additional clocks are required for each Address Absolute mode to read the address.

Additional clocks are required for each Address Absolute mode and is dependent on the operand size. More clocks will be required to write the result if the destination mode is Address Absolute but only those required to do the actual write since the address is already known.

For those processors that allow relative addressing, there must also be a way to force the assembler to use an absolute address instead. This is the case for memory mapped I/O registers.

There will usually be some special notation which tells the assembler that the value is an absolute address rather than a relative one or even an immediate value.

Example:

```
COPY.2    (0xFFFF1234), R0    ; read the contents of address
                              ; 0xFFFF1234 and put the value
                              ; into R0
```

Without the () the instruction might put the value 0xFFFF1234 into R0 depending on the assembler syntax.

Total execution time is 4 clocks:

1 = read the COPY instruction
2 = read 4 byte address
1 = read 2 byte operand one
0 = store value in R0

Total memory usage is 6 bytes:

2 bytes for the ADD instruction
4 bytes for the operand address

Example:

```
JMPA      Function_11      ; jump to the function which is named
                           ; Function_11
```

The assembler recognizes the JMPA instruction as "jump absolute." In this case the address of Function_11 will be the final bytes of the instruction. The number of bytes required for the address will be dependent on the architecture of the processor. Essentially what happens is that the address of Function_11 is placed into the four bytes immediately following the JMPA opcode.

Total execution time is:

1 = read the JMP instruction
2 = read 4 byte address
1 = copy the address into the Program Counter

Total memory usage:

2 bytes for the ADD instruction
4 bytes for the address

IMPORTANT: If the processor supports both Address Relative and Address Absolute modes, the assembler must have some way in its syntax to differentiate between them.

For the PDP11 and VAX computers the syntax is:

```
MOV       R0, Address      ; argument two is Address Relative

MOV       R0, @#Address    ; argument two is Address Absolute
```

The result of both instructions is identical. The Address Absolute mode is usually used only for accessing the I/O registers. See chapter 5 for details on accessing I/O.

4
This Processor

Basic Processor Features

This book develops a fictional processor. This decision was made in order to keep this from becoming a book about a specific processor and whatever limitations it may have. This also gives the freedom to create whatever instructions and features are necessary for the various topics. However, there is an obvious disadvantage – you will not be able to run the sample programs, although you will be able to assemble them using the assembler that is available. You should be able to take the techniques learned and apply them to any processor.

Here is a summary of the architecture features of the processor which is discussed in this book:

- von Neumann memory architecture
- CISC
- Orthogonal Instruction Set
- Little Endian
- 2's-complement binary arithmetic
- Floating point hardware
- Memory Mapped I/O
- 16 bit internal data bus
- 32 bit Program Counter and Stack Pointer
- 16 bit Processor Status Register

- 16 sets of four 64 bit general purpose registers
  - the registers may be used as 8, 16, 32 and 64 bits
- 8 interrupt levels, prioritized, each with a dedicated register set
- Dedicated vector address in low memory for each interrupt
- Program Counter and Processor Status Register pushed onto stack for interrupts
- When the processor comes out of Reset
  - The IPL is set to 7, effectively disabling interrupts
  - The content of address 0 (4 bytes) is placed into the Program Counter

These are the features, or their equivalents for your specific processor, that you need to thoroughly understand before attempting to program any microprocessor.

This chapter describes the basic architecture of the processor with other features described in chapters related specifically to those features. Many of the features have been selected from the perspective of the processor being primarily designed for embedded systems.

One of the basic ways to describe a processor and its features is to start with its "number of bits". This is a 16 bit processor with a 32 bit Program Counter. Keeping the data bus to 16 bits allows it to use less expensive memories, as compared to a 32 bit processor, and to keep the number of pins required for the memory interface to a relatively small value without resorting to many memory cycles per instruction.

There were essentially only two other practical choices for this feature: 8 bits and 32 bits. The 8 bit architecture was eliminated because I want to build an instruction set which more efficiently handles 16 and 32 bit data values. I eliminated 32 bits because I did not want to be forced to have instructions which, in general, would be multiples of 32 bits. I believe 16 bits yields a very efficient processor with a relatively low cost to implement.

Along with the 16 bit data bus is the requirement that all instructions be multiples of 16 bits. A side effect of this is that all instructions begin on even numbered byte addresses. This will cause some inefficiencies in the instruction set due to some values needing an odd number of bytes – primarily strings. However, I believe that this is a relatively minor issue. In earlier processors, think 8080 and 6800, using an 8 bit architecture was extremely important due in large part to the cost of memory. I remember having to pay upwards of $1000 for an 8 KB memory!

Given the technology of today, the choice of a 32 bit Program Counter is almost a "given" for any processor used in anything other than very small applications. Although there are many processors with smaller PCs (many PICs, for instance) they are usually for applications that have a relatively small program space requirement. Many 8 and 16 bit processors with 16 bit PCs use memory management techniques to expand the program memory space beyond 16 bits. Assembly Language can be hard enough without having to deal with these limitations. I have chosen to implement an Orthogonal Instruction Set based on sets of four 64 bit registers. Most of the instructions allow using the 4 registers interchangeably. There are a limited number of instructions which use dedicated registers.

Interrupts

Eight of the register sets (RS0 – RS7) are essentially dedicated to the eight interrupt levels. This allows the programmer to have at least 4 registers that do not need to be saved and restored during the execution of the Interrupt Service Routine. This feature allows for more efficient (read that as "faster") ISRs. The eight interrupt levels are prioritized such that an interrupt will be serviced only if its priority is higher than the current Interrupt Priority Level. Typically, the processor is operating at IPL0 and is using Register Set 0.

When an interrupt is acknowledged by the processor both the PC and PSR are pushed onto the stack, in that order. This allows for an essentially unlimited number of interrupts. Practically the limit is closer to seven. When the Return from Interrupt instruction is executed the PSR and PC are restored from the stack.

Here are a few reasons why the processor may not acknowledge an interrupt event:

> Interrupts for that event are not enabled.
>
> The processor is executing at a higher Interrupt Priority Level.
>
> The event may be too short. This can happen if the processor allows external events as interrupts. These events must be synchronized with the CPU clock via some internal logic that requires the event to be at least some number of CPU clock cycles in length.

The vector table for this processor resides in the first 1024 (0x400) bytes of the memory. Each entry is a single 32 bit value which is the address of the associated ISR. Since each entry is four bytes, this allows for 256 vectors. For an embedded system this should be plenty. Obviously, since this is a fictional processor, the number of vectors can easily be increased. Address 0x00000000 contains the starting address of the program – you can think of this as the start-up interrupt vector, the only difference is that it does not push any values onto the stack.

Here is a detailed analysis of what happens when an interrupt is acknowledged. The value at the start of each line is the number of clocks required:

- X – current instruction has to complete – this can be as long as 17 clocks (floating point divide)
- 3 – push the current PC onto the stack
  - 1 – decrement the SP by four
  - 2 – copy the PC (4 bytes) to the stack
- 2 – push the PSR onto the stack
  - 1 – decrement SP by two
  - 1 – copy the PSR (2 bytes) to the stack
- 0 – "create" new PSR value based on the IPL
- 2 – retrieve the ISR address from the interrupt vector
- 1 – put the ISR address into the PC

The total number of clocks is X+8. This "delay" in reaching the ISR is called interrupt latency.

The ISR must exit using the RETI instruction which will pull the previous PSR and PC from the stack:

- 2 – pull the PSR from the stack
  - 1 – copy the value from the stack to the PSR
  - 1 – increment the SP by two
- 3 – pull the PC from the stack
  - 2 – copy the value from the stack to the PC
  - 1 – increment the SP by four

Total interrupt overhead is the sum of the two values: X + 8 + 5 = X + 13. Whenever calculating interrupt processing time you need to add this expression to the total time.

Memory Layout

In general there will be a limited discussion of Memory Management techniques in this book. However, I do need to define the memory addressing scheme used. The processor uses Memory Mapped I/O for both internal and external register accesses. The upper bits of the address are used to determine the memory being accessed as follows:

- 0000 0000 – FFFD FFFF is program and data space
- FFFE 0000 – FFFE FFFF is external I/O (65KB)
- FFFF 0000 – FFFF FFFF is internal I/O (65KB)

Since this book is about Assembly Language, it is not going to discuss any further details associated with accessing memory. Things such as Chip Selects, Output Enables and Read Enable signals are not necessary for the purposes of this book. However, you may need to become familiar with them when programming your specific processor.

The following chart shows the memory layout for this processor. You will notice in the sample programs that there are several values used for the start of RAM but always the same value for the start of the program. The hardware in this processor forces an address for the start of flash but does not do the same for RAM.

The "?? MB" for both the flash and RAM indicate that the values are implementation dependent.

Fig. 4.1

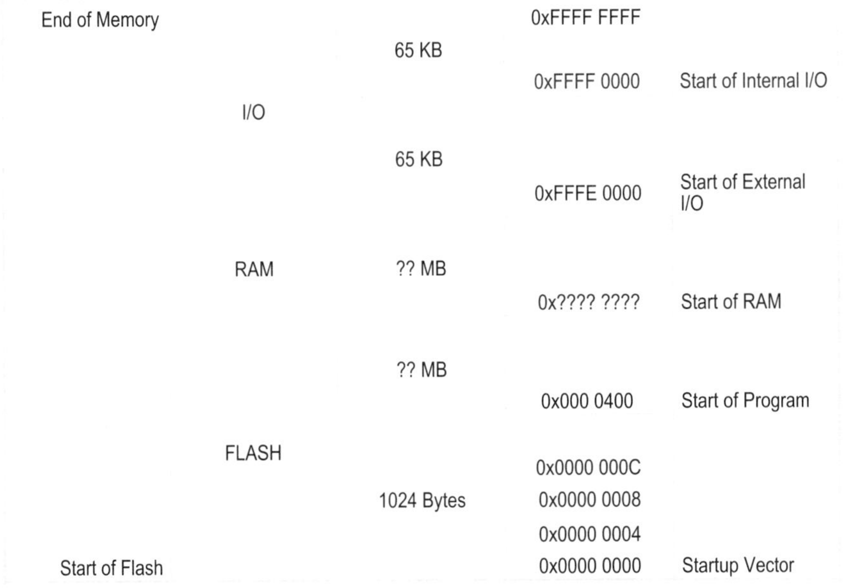

Processor Status Register

The PSR contains the following fields:

- Condition Code Bits (4 bits)
- Current register set: RS0 ... RS15 (4 bits decoded)
- Current IPL: 0 ... 7 (3 bits decoded)
- Startup Method (3 bits decoded)
  - Power-up
  - RESET while powered
  - Watchdog Timer timeout
  - Software

The PSR will be pushed onto the stack (after the PC) whenever an interrupt is acknowledged by the processor but before the new IPL and register set number are stored into it.

The Watchdog Timer is a device which can be used by the programmer to cause an interrupt or reset if it is not "petted" before it times out. The timeout value is usually programmable. The purpose of the timer is to reset the processor should the program ever get into an infinite loop. Since this feature does not have anything specifically with assembly language there will be no further discussion about it.

Condition Codes

As previously mentioned, the condition codes used in this processor are:

- Negative
- Zero
- Carry
- Overflow

These will often be referred to by the letters N, Z, C and V followed by "-bit".

Any computer program will have to make many decisions during its execution. It is the condition codes which enable these decisions to be made. A thorough understanding of how these work is necessary to successfully program in Assembly Language for any processor. In general for this processor the condition codes are affected by all arithmetic and logical instructions. This is not the case for all processors; for example the 8080 and its derivatives.

In much of the discussion of these bits, as well as elsewhere in this book, the term "set" means "on" or a value of one. The term "cleared" means "off" or a value of 0. It should also be noted that any given operation may set and/or clear more than one of the condition codes.

The N-bit is simply a replication of the Most Significant Bit of the result of the instruction just executed. The N-bit is set if the MSB is set and cleared if it is cleared. Another way of stating this if signed arithmetic is being used is: the N-bit is set if the result is negative and cleared if the result is positive. Keep in mind that the MSB of a signed value is the sign bit when 2's-complement arithmetic is being used. A few examples using the ADD instruction should be sufficient to show this. First a brief explanation of the ADD instruction: perform an arithmetic addition of the operands and place the result in the location specified by the second argument, replacing the original value.

```
ADD.1     R0, R1     ; R1 = R0 + R1 using only bits 0..7
                     ; (1 byte as indicated by the ".1" suffix)
```

The following table shows the N-bit value following the execution of several ADD.1 instructions:

Fig. 4.2

Before		After	
R0	R1	R1	N
1	1	2	0
–1	–1	–2	1
1	–1	0	0
127	1	–128	1

You may find the last example to be confusing. Since the instruction specified 8 bit operands, the largest positive signed integer value is 127. Adding one to this value yields a hexadecimal value of 0x80 which is –128 in 2's-complement binary using 8 bit data. For unsigned arithmetic the result would still be 0x80 but would be interpreted as +128. Even so, the most significant bit is still set; therefore, the N-bit would still be set.

The Z-bit is even easier. It is set when the result of the operation yields a value of 0 in the destination location. It is cleared otherwise. Note that the Z-bit can be set even if the C-bit is set by the operation. However, it is impossible for both the Z-bit and N-bit to be set at the same time.

The C-bit can be used for extended precision arithmetic. It is set if the result of the operation requires one more bit than is available for the size of the data being used. This enables a processor to operate on values that are larger than what the register set typically handles. For instance, if you are adding two 8 bit values, using 8 bit registers, and the result cannot be contained within 8 bits; that is, any value within the range 256 to 510. The following discussion and table, using 8 bit registers, show an example in detail of when single registers are too small to hold the result of two values being added. In general, the lesser significant portions of the values are handled as *unsigned* values while the most significant portion is handled as a *signed* value – unless the values themselves are unsigned then each portion is handled as *unsigned*.

Adding 358 to 2265 yields 2623. The values are too large to fit into 8 bit registers so it takes the concatenation of two registers to hold each value. To add them you need to add the LSBytes first: R1 + R3. Note that the addition of the two LSBytes generates a Carry. The next operation adds the Carry bit to the MSbyte of one of the values: R0 + C (it does not matter which one). Then the two MSbytes (R0 + R2) are added yielding the final result. Of course it is also possible that adding the C-bit to the register could itself generate a carry and/or this final addition could also generate a carry. It is up to the programmer to determine how far to "carry" this procedure.

Fig. 4.3

The combination of R0 ans R1 contains the number 358

The combination of R2 and R3 contains the number 2265

				R0				C					R1			
0	0	0	0	0	0	0	1		0	1	1	0	0	1	1	0
				R2									R3			
0	0	0	0	1	0	0	0		1	1	0	1	1	0	0	1
													R1 = R1 + R3			
								1	0	0	1	1	1	1	1	1
				R0 = R0 + C												
0	0	0	0	0	0	1	0									
				R0 + R2									R1 = R1 + R3			
0	0	0	0	1	0	1	0		0	0	1	1	1	1	1	1

The assembly language statements for these operations are as follows:

```
add.l     R3, R1    ; add the LSBytes
addc.l    R0        ; update one of the MSBytes with the Carry
                    ; from the previous operation
add.      R2, R0    ; add the MSBytes
```

Note that the sequence does not check the C-bit to determine whether or not the addc needs to be executed. If the C-bit is not set by the first add operation, the addc will have no effect on the sequence.
This mechanism is also used with subtraction where the C-bit is used as an indication of a borrow operation. Instead of adding the C-bit to the MSbyte you would subtract it. You need to keep in mind that although these examples have used bytes as the basic data size, all of this discussion applies just as well to other data sizes.

Another circumstance for using the C bit is for determining the state of bit 0. You can execute a rotate instruction that will move bit 0 into the C-bit. The next instruction would probably be a branch that is conditional upon the state of the C-bit. There are other ways of testing the state of bit 0 but they take up more memory and clock cycles.

The V-bit indicates an overflow condition for signed integer arithmetic operations. The V-bit will be set if the signs of the two operands are the same but the result of the operation yields a value with the opposite sign. In other words, adding two positive values yields a negative result or adding two negative values yields a positive result. This can be expressed using Boolean arithmetic as follows:

$$V = (S1 \text{ xor } S2) \text{ xor } S3$$

Where S1 and S2 are the signs of the two operands and S3 is the sign of the result.

The following table shows the V-bit value following the addition of two 1 byte values:

```
add.l    R0, R1
```

Fig. 4.4

Before		After	
R0	R1	R1	V
1	1	2	0
–1	–1	–2	0
1	–1	0	0
127	1	–128	1
–120	–10	126	1

Current Register Set

Since this processor has 16 sets of registers and each IPL has its own set, there needs to be a way to store the register set number (abbreviated as RSn) when an interrupt occurs. That mechanism is the PSR. There are 4 bits in the PSR which maintain the "current" register set number. When an interrupt occurs, the PSR gets pushed onto the stack and the new register set number for the interrupt is inserted into the PSR. When the ISR exits, the previous PSR gets restored from the stack.

The instruction that allows the program to change which register set is being used causes the register set number to be stored into the PSR.

Interrupt Priority Level

This processor implements a typical interrupt priority mechanism. An interrupt will not be acknowledged by the processor, unless its priority is higher than the current processor priority. The processor is normally operating at IPL = 0, so any device that can interrupt will be acknowledged. If the processor is executing at IPL = 4, only an interrupt that has an IPL of five or greater will be acknowledged. Interrupts with IPLs of 4 or lower will not be lost, but they will have to wait until all the higher priority interrupts have completed.

Even within those devices that have identical IPLs there will be a priority. For example, if two devices with the same IPL interrupt at the same time, how does the processor determine which one gets acknowledged? There will have to be a hardware priority mechanism which makes that determination.

Programmer's Model

The diagram of Figure 4.5 is what is often referred to as a Programmer's Model of this processor. In general, the Programmer's Model is simply a pictorial representation of the CPU registers. It does not include the I/O registers.

Fig. 4.5

Program Counter		31	30	...	1	0						
Stack Pointer		31	30	...	1	0						
Processor Status Register		0	0	StartUp			---IPL---	---RS---	N	C	V	Z
Registers	RS0:R0	63...0		31...0			15...0	7...0				
	RS0:R1	63...0		31...0			15...0	7...0				
	RS0:R2	63...0		31...0			15...0	7...0				
	RS0:R3	63...0		31...0			15...0	7...0				
	RS1:R0	63...0		31...0			15...0	7...0				
	...											
	...											
	RS15:R0	63...0		31...0			15...0	7...0				
	RS15:R1	63...0		31...0			15...0	7...0				
	RS15:R2	63...0		31...0			15...0	7...0				
	RS15:R3	63...0		31...0			15...0	7...0				

Note that for this processor the general registers can be accessed in any of four sizes: 8, 16, 32 or 64 bits.

Address Modes

The address modes for this processor and their syntax is shown here along with a single example for each. When using a register as an argument, only the lowest bytes are used; the remaining bytes are not affected.

The number of bytes is defined by the number specified in the instruction. In these examples the value is always two.

Register – Both arguments are register mode. The register content is the operand.

```
copy.2   R0, R1
```

Register Indirect – Argument one is Register Indirect mode. The register content is the address of the operand.

```
copy.2   (R0), R1
```

Offset – Argument one is Offset mode. The sum of the register content and the *2 byte* offset is the address of the operand. If an offset value larger than can fit into two bytes is attempted, the assembler will generate a warning and insert a truncated value.

```
copy.2   1234(R0), R1
```

Immediate – For most instructions only argument one can be Immediate mode. The operand is a 1, 2, 4 or 8 byte numeric value whose size is dependent on the number of bytes specified by the instruction. The special prefix character "#" is required. If an operand value larger than is specified by the instruction suffix is attempted, the assembler will generate a warning and insert a truncated value.

```
copy.2   #1234, R1
```

Address Absolute – argument two is Address Absolute mode. The address of the operand (4 bytes) follows the instruction.

```
copy.2   R0, Value1
```

5
I/O Devices

The internal I/O space is used to access registers that control various hardware features of the processor such as:

- Processor speed options
- Memory speed and access parameters
- Bootstrap/start-up options
- I/O devices such as parallel ports, serial ports, timers, etc.

Only the I/O devices have much to do with learning Assembly Language. The other items in the list have more to do with configuring the processor hardware architecture. This section will detail a few I/O devices which will be used in some of the sample code and exercises. Each device is described as to its functions, limitations and, in some cases, advantages.

Of most importance to the programmer are the registers each device uses. In many cases, one can completely describe the functionality of a device by understanding the registers and how to use them. All of the I/O registers will have an "x" in their name. This value represents the device number to handle the case where there are multiple units of identical devices. In the sample programs, it will be replaced with a single digit. Also, there will be some notation that looks like: ABxCDE:y. This represents a *register.bit* combination.

Many of the registers have multiple uses. Since they can be accessed in the same way as memory, the program can use the same instructions to access them – including those that operate on single bits. The importance of this will be seen as you review the registers.

Some of the sample programs will require you to refer to these registers. Also, this is the first time in this book where the I/O register names are being used. These names are the method by which the samples and the exercises will refer to the registers. The assembler comes with a header file, Processor_Definitions.h, that defines all the internal I/O register names and addresses as well as the interrupt vectors. You will also have to be aware of the size of each of the registers – they vary in size based on the particular parameters being set and/or read. Although there was an attempt to make these registers as complete as possible, there is the possibility that there are some control/status values missing. Immediately following the name will be three characteristics of the port:

- The size of the register in bytes
- An indication of the allowable access to the register:
  - R/W = read and write
  - R = read only
  - W = write only
- The Reset value
  - ? = random

It will be assumed that there can be at least eight each ($0 \leq x \leq 7$) of the devices described in this chapter. Also, actually implementing the degree of selection shown in the registers for these I/O devices is probably not practical. Most microprocessors will have several of each type and a way of selecting which is to be used.

Something else to be aware of regarding I/O registers is that a single address could possibly refer to a 32 bit register. It is not necessary that a "4 byte" register have four addresses. This processor does allocate multiple addresses to multi-byte registers simply because that is what you will typically find. However, it is not strictly necessary.

The devices described here are:

- Parallel Ports
- Serial Ports
- Timer/Counters
- Pulse Modulators

There are many more I/O devices which are not discussed here such as:

- DMA
- Analog to Digital Convertors (A/D)
- Digital to Analog Convertors (D/A)
- Ethernet
- USB

Discussing the four devices listed should be sufficient for learning how to program I/O devices via Assembly Language, rather than the functions available in high level languages. If you have not seen this level of detail before, you will gain an appreciation of the work that goes into developing the functions available in those languages.

The I/O devices are memory mapped as stated earlier. This means any instruction that can access memory can just as easily access the I/O registers in the same way. However, in order to be more efficient, other instructions have been implemented that allow the program to access the I/O registers with shorter instructions. These additional instructions allow the I/O address to be shortened to 16 bits instead of the 32 bits required for a memory address. See the IOCOPY, IOOR and IOAND instructions in the Instruction Set chapter.

Parallel Ports

There are eight parallel ports in this processor.

Parallel ports are the workhorse of microprocessor based control systems. Most microprocessors today have several parallel ports with varying capabilities. Most allow the ports to have several programmable features such as:

- Direction
  - Input or output
- Drive current for outputs
  - How much current each output bit can sink and/or source
- Open drain for outputs
  - As opposed to a standard CMOS output, basically remove the upper transistor from the output circuit.
- Input load
  - Place a resistor on the input to either power or ground
- Selectable output function
  - Choose from among several output functions

The parallel ports in this processor have all of these features. Most are self explanatory but the "selectable I/O function" may take some explaining. Most microprocessors today have many built-in hardware features such as those listed in the previous section. In many cases these I/O devices do not have dedicated pins assigned to them – they get their pins from the parallel ports. Those features which are inputs are generally controlled by the registers associated with that feature. The features which are outputs are selected by the parallel port configuration registers. Again, this will become clear as the registers are described.

Parallel Port Registers

PPxDATA – (1 byte, R/W, ?) Parallel Port **x** Data Register

Writing to this register will set the state of every bit which has its Function code set to one, see **PPxCFG** and **PPx.yCFG**. Reading this register will return the state of every bit – independent of the function.

PPxCFG – (1 byte, R/W, 0) Parallel Port **x** Default Configuration Register.

This register may be used to set all of the bits of the port to the same configuration. The **PPx.yCFG** registers are used if you want to configure specific bits differently. Programming these registers is sequence sensitive in that writing to this register, **PPxCFG**, will cause its value to be propagated to each of the **PPx.yCFG** registers.

Fig. 5.1

Bit(s)	7	6	5, 4	3	2, 1, 0
Input	*Load Value* 0 = 100 K 1= 20 K	0	*Load* 00 = pulldown 01 = pullup 10 = keeper 11 = none	0	*Function* 000 = Input 001 = PPxDATA 010 = use bit 3 for state
Output	*Slew Rate* 0 = Slow 1 = Fast	*Output Type* 0 = CMOS 1 = Open Drain	*Current* 00 = 4 mA 01 = 8 mA 10 = 12 mA 11 = 16 mA	0	

- Reset Value: 0x00 = all bits as inputs with a 100K pulldown
- Load Value: Input: Selects between two load resistor values
- Load: Input: Selects how the load resistor is connected to the input

  The "Keeper" selection connects the input, through the Load Value resistance, to the output of a circuit which is the last value applied to the input. This gives the input the capability of hysteresis.
- Slew Rate: Output: Selects how fast the signal rises and falls.

Output Type: Output: Selects the output configuration.

0 = Standard CMOS output which is driven both high and low.

1 = Open Drain to ground.

Current: Output: Selects the drive current capability.

Function: Selects from among three available functions for the port.

0 = all bits are inputs and are read via **PPxDATA**

1 = all bits are outputs and are written via **PPxDATA**

2 = all bits are outputs and are programmed individually via **PPx.yCFG:3**

Here are two sample Configuration Register values using hexadecimal and binary:

All bits are Input with a pullup of 20K

= 0x00 + 0x10 + 0x80 = 0x90

= 0b10010000

All bits are Output using **PPxData**, 12ma drive, open drain, slow rise

= 0x01 + 0x20 + 0x40 + 0x00 = 0x61

= 0b01100001

PPx.yCFG – (1 byte, R/W, 0) Parallel Port **x** Bit **y** Configuration Register.

Each parallel port (**x**) has eight bits and each bit (y) has a dedicated configuration register. These registers are used to completely configure the port bits. Configuring the parallel ports is one of the first operations executed in an embedded system – probably right after setting up the memory. It is usually good technique to put all of the configuration code in a function and to call it from the main program.

Notice that the Reset Value (see below) sets all the bits to inputs with a pulldown. This is done to ensure that the processor does not attempt to drive a signal into a device which is driving the processor (two devices driving the same point) and to ensure that there are no floating inputs – not good for CMOS devices.

Fig. 5.2

Bit(s)	7	6	5, 4	3	2, 1, 0
	Load Value		*Load*		
	0 = 100 K		00 = pulldown		
Input	1= 20 K	0	01 = pullup	0	
			10 = keeper		*Function*
			11 = none		000 = Input
	Slew Rate	*Output Type*	*Current*	*State*	001 = PPxDATA
	0 = Slow	0 = CMOS	00 = 4 mA	0/1	010 = use bit 3 for state
Output	1 = Fast	1 = Open Drain	01 = 8 mA	(only if	011-111= output function
			10 = 12 mA	function =	
			11 = 16 mA	010)	

Reset Value: 0x00 = all bits as inputs with a 100K pulldown

Load Value: Input: Selects between two load resistor values.

Load: Input: Selects how the load resistor is connected.
The "Keeper" selection connects the input, through Load Value resistance, to the output of a circuit which is the last value applied to the input. This gives the input the capability of hysteresis.

Slew Rate: Output: Selects how fast the output signal rises and falls.

Output Type: Output: Selects the output configuration.

0 = Standard CMOS output which is driven both high and low.

1 = Open Drain to ground.

Current: Output: Selects the drive current capability.

State: Output: Bit state if Function = 010

Function: Selects from among eight available functions for the pin.

0 = This bit is an input and is read via **PPxDATA**

1 = This bit is an output and is written via **PPxDATA**

2 = This bit is an output and is programmed via bit 3

3–7 = select from among five different output devices such as:

Serial port transmitters
Pulse modulator outputs
See *Sample Port Assignments* later in this chapter

There are no interrupts associated with the parallel ports. Although, if the processor allowed external signals to generate interrupts, those signals would come through parallel port bits so you would want to make those bits inputs.

Serial Ports

There are eight serial ports in this processor.

A USART, Universal Synchronous/Asynchronous Receiver/Transmitter, is another one of the more basic I/O devices used in microprocessors today. The type of asynchronous device discussed here is the typical device found in many PCs today, although they are becoming more rare due to the utilization of USB ports. They have been around since the early 1950's. Without going into a lot of detail, the earliest versions I used operated at 110 baud. The teletype devices used in the 1940's were 50 baud and did not use UARTs. Today, speeds in excess of 1Mbaud are available – assuming the associated hardware can handle it. There are other serial protocols such as Ethernet, USB, CAN, etc. but they have special hardware which is not generally considered to be a USART.

There are a number of parameters which need to be set in order for the USART to operate properly. All devices connected to the communications channel must use the same values for those parameters. In its asynchronous mode, a USART is often used as an RS232 or RS485 device. For both of those protocols, there must be some hardware external to the processor to interface with the other units. *Never* connect an RS232 signal directly to a microprocessor – you will kill at least one of the pins and possibly the entire processor. RS232 voltages range from at least -6V to +6V.

One of the hardware features of a USART is that the transmitter data is buffered as shown in this diagram:

Fig. 5.3

When data is written to the Transmit Data Register (TDR), it is held there until the Transmit Shift Register (TSR) is empty. If the TSR is empty when the TDR is written, the data will transfer immediately. Data shifts out of the TSR one bit at a time. This feature enables a continuous stream of bits to be transmitted because the program has an entire byte transmit time in which to load the next byte into the TDR.

The receiver is buffered in a similar manor:

Fig. 5.4

When the Receive Shift Register (RSR) has completed receiving a byte, it is transferred to the Receive Data Register (RDR). This leaves an entire byte time for the microprocessor to take the byte from the RDR. If another byte is received before the byte is read from the RDR, an error condition will occur which is called *overflow* and the byte is lost. Some processors have a First-In-First-Out (FIFO) memory for the RDR. In this case several bytes can accumulate in the FIFO before an overflow occurs. This is very handy when operating at higher baud rates where one byte-time may not always be enough for the processor to retrieve a byte from the RDR.

Asynchronous Mode

Asynchronous serial communications using a USART usually incurs a 20% overhead: 8 data bits plus the start and stop bits. The "extra" bits are what allows the receiving device to synchronize with the transmitting device. In general, the baud rates between the transmitting and receiving devices can be different by up to almost 10% and still have reliable communications. This is not so important now since crystal oscillators are usually used as the baud rate generators. However, this was not always the case. In the "early" days of computers the baud rates were controlled by RC circuits and were prone to drift as well as inaccuracies.

Some features of Asynchronous mode are:

- Transmits and receives the Least Significant Bit first
- The idle state is a "mark" or logic 1
- The start bit is a "space" or logic 0
- The stop bit is a "mark"
- A parity bit is optional

  Parity is a method of error detection that forces the number of 1's in the byte to be either even or odd. For instance, a byte value of 0x55 has four 1's and four 0's. If odd parity is being used, the transmitter will append an extra 1 in the parity position in order to force an odd number of "1" bits. If even parity being used, the parity bit will be a 0.

- Can be 7 or 8 data bits
- An optional 9th bit can be used to indicate data vs. address in some protocols
- It is a Non-Return-to-Zero (NRZ) protocol
- The receiving device usually samples the incoming data stream 8 or 16 times per bit. This must be taken into account when calculating the divisor for the baud rate generator.

Synchronous Mode

The synchronous mode is SPI, a protocol invented by Motorola in the 1960s, which allows a single serial port to communicate with several I/O devices – usually on the same circuit board. In most cases, devices communicating via SPI can be connected directly to the processor.

Some features of the Synchronous mode are:

- Transmits and receives the Most Significant Bit first
- There is no standard idle state
- The standard is 8 data bits although there are some non-standard "SPI" devices which use more than 8
- It is also a Non-Return-to-Zero (NRZ) protocol
- Uses a clock signal – hence the name "synchronous"
- Is a Master/Slave system
- The Master always generates the clock – even when the Slave is transmitting
- The Master enables the Slave via a Chip Select line
- The transmitting device starts a bit on one edge of the clock and the receiving device latches it on the next edge

There are four signals used for most SPI devices. The first three are common to all devices on the network. The fourth is the chip select and is unique per Slave device. Only the device with the active Chip Select is enabled to communicate with the Master.

The Chip Select will be active during the entire transaction. The common signal are:

- MOSI – Master Out Slave In – Master Transmitter to Slave Receiver(s)
- MISO – Master In Slave Out – Master Receiver to Slave Transmitter(s)
- Clock – always generated by the Master

The diagram of Figure 5.5 may be helpful:

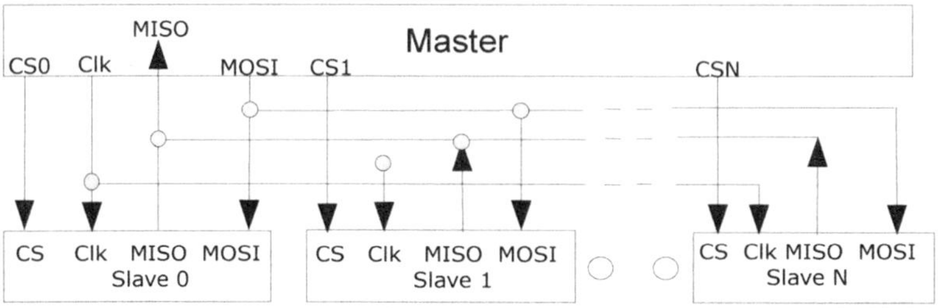

Fig. 5.5

Some examples of SPI devices are:

- A/D convertors
- D/A convertors
- serial flash memories

USART Registers

SPxDATA – (2 bytes, R/W, ?) Serial Port **x** Data Register

This register handles both the received and transmitted data. In order to transmit for either mode, all that needs to be done is to write the data to the register. If eight or fewer bits are being transmitted, then just write to the low byte of the register. To transmit more than eight bits, write to the register as a word (two bytes). For the Asynchronous and SPI Master modes, the byte will be transmitted immediately. For the SPI Slave mode, the byte will be transmitted when the SPI Master requests it. In all cases the **TxBufEmpty** bit in **SPxSTAT** will get set when the byte transfers from the TDR to the TSR. The **TxBusy** bit is set as long as the transmitter is busy shifting out bits, or waiting for the clock from the SPI Master, and gets cleared when it is idle. If more than 8 bits are being used in SPI mode, the LSB is bit 0 of the lower byte. Bit 0 of the high byte is also the 9th bit, if used, in the Asynchronous mode.

SPxDIV – (2 bytes, R/W, 0) Serial Port **x** Divisor Register

This register is the divisor for generating the baud/bit rate. The divider is driven from the CPU clock or an external clock and always divides by the register value +1 so the divisor can never be 0. The USART in its *Asynchronous* mode samples each bit 16 times so the formula for the baud rate is:

Clock / 16 / (**SPxDIV** + 1)

The USART in its *Synchronous* mode divides the clock by two so the bit rate calculation is:

Clock / 2 / (**SPxDIV** + 1)

SPxRPORT – (1 byte, R/W, 0) Serial Port **x** Receive Port

Fig. 5.6

Bit(s)	7	6, 5, 4	3	2, 1, 0
	1 = Start Rx	Parallel Port	0	Bit nbr

Reset Value: 0x00

StartRx: Synch: Start a receive operation for the SPI mode when the processor is the Master device. The operation of setting the bit causes the byte receive operation to start by initiating the clock signal. The bit does not have to be cleared.

Parallel Port: The parallel port for the Rx bit

Bit nbr: The bit within the parallel port for the Rx bit

*Note: the transmit port is selected via the appropriate **PPx.yCFG***

SPxCFG – (1 byte, R/W, 0x10) Serial Port **x** Configuration Register

Fig. 5.7

Bit(s)	7	6	5, 4	3, 2, 1, 0
		Stop Bits	*Data Bits*	*Parity*
Asynch	0	0 = 1 1 = 2	00 = 7 01 = 8 10 = 9 11 = nu	0000 = none 0100 = even 0101 = odd 0110 = space 0111 = mark
Synch (SPI)	1	0 = Master 1 = Slave	*Clock Mode* see Table	number of bits

Reset value: 0x10 = Asynchronous, 1 stop bit, 8 data bits, no parity

Asynchronous Mode – bit 7 = 0

Stop Bits: Select the number of start bits for each byte

- Parity: Select the parity for each byte
- Data Bits: Select the number of data bits

Synchronous Mode – bit 7 = 1

- Mode: Select either Master or Slave operation
- Nbr of Bits: Select the number of bits for SPI data

These bits allow the synchronous mode to handle any number of bits from 1 to 15. The vast majority of SPI devices use multiples of eight bits, but I have encountered a few instances that do not.

- Clock Mode: Select from among the 4 clock-to-data phase relationships. See the SPI Timing Table.

In general, it is best to compare the timing requirements of the Slave device(s) with the table and select the appropriate clock mode. If you need to communicate with devices requiring different modes, the register can be modified during program execution to select the appropriate clock mode as needed.

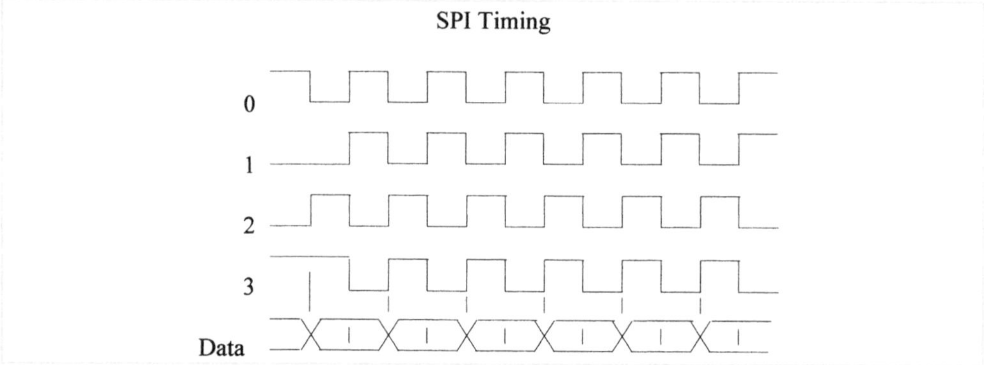

Fig. 5.8

The vertical bars within the Data values indicates when the receiving device should latch the data.

The other vertical bars indicate when the transmitting device applies a new value to the data bus. This leaves half a clock period for the data to settle before being clocked into the receiving device.

Here are two sample Configuration Register values using hexadecimal and binary:

Asynch, 2 stop bits, 8 data bits, even parity

= 0x00 + 0x40 + 0x10 + 0x04 = 0x54

= 0b01010100

Synchronous, Master, Mode = 2, 8 data bits

= 0x80 + 0x40 + 0x20 + 0x08 = 0xE8

= 0b11101000

SPxCLK – (1 byte, R/W, 0) Serial Port **x** Clock Source

This register is used for both the Asynchronous and the SPI Slave modes. For the SPI Master mode, the I/O pin for the clock is selected via **PPx.yCFG**. If an external clock is selected, it is handled the same as the CPUclock and is subject to the same processing via SPxDIV. If an external clock is used its frequency must be less than CPUclock/4 in order to allow synchronization with internal logic.

Fig. 5.9

Bit(s)	7	6, 5, 4	3	2, 1, 0
	Clock 0 = Int 1 = Ext	Parallel Port	0	Bit nbr

Reset Value: 0x00

Clock: Select the clock source for the USART

0 = use CPU clock – not valid for SPI slave

1 = use clock from selected parallel port input.

Parallel Port: Select the parallel port for the clock

Bit nbr: Select the bit of the parallel port for the clock

SPxINT – (1 byte, R/W, 0) Serial Port **x** Interrupt Register

Fig. 5.10

Bit(s)	7	6, 5, 4	3	2, 1, 0
	TxBusy	TxIPL	0	RxIPL

Reset Value: 0x00

TxBusy: Enable interrupt when **SPxSTAT:TxBusy** transitions from 1 to 0

TxIPL: Interrupt Priority Level, 0 = interrupts disabled

RxIPL: Receive Interrupt Priority Level, 0 = interrupts disabled

The interrupt vector names for the serial ports are **VECTOR_SPxTX** and **VECTOR_SPxRX** where the "**x**" is replaced by the Serial Port number. If transmit interrupts are enabled, an interrupt will be generated every time a byte moves from the TDR to the TSR.

Setting **SPxINT:TxBusy** enables an interrupt to occur when the last bit has completed. This can be handy for systems where you might want to disable the transmitter circuit after the last byte has completed, for instance in RS485 systems.

SPxSTAT – (1 byte, R, 0) Serial Port **x** Status Register

Fig. 5.11

Bit	7	6	5	4	3	2	1	0
	1 = TxBusy	1 = TxBuf Empty	0	0	1 = RxDone	1 = RxParity	1 = Rx Overrun	0

Reset Value: 0x00

TxBusy: Set while the transmitter is busy shifting out bits.

Cleared when the last bit has completed. If transmit interrupts are enabled and the ***SPxINT:TxBusy*** *is set the transition from 1 to 0 will cause an interrupt. The interrupt condition is cleared when the interrupt is serviced.*

TxBufEmpty: Set when the TDR transfers its data to the TSR.

If transmit interrupts are enabled this event will cause an interrupt. The data register can be loaded with new data at this time. The bit is cleared when the register is read or when a new value is written to ***SPxDATA****. The interrupt condition is cleared when the interrupt is serviced.*

RxDone: Set when a byte has been received and is in SPxDATA.

If receive interrupts are enabled this event will cause an interrupt. The bit is cleared when ***SPxDATA*** *is read. The interrupt condition is cleared when the interrupt is serviced.*

RxParity: Asynch only – Set when a parity error has been detected in a received byte.

*This bit is valid only if a parity value has been selected in **SPxCFG**. The bit is cleared when the register is read.*

RxOverrun: Set when a byte is received and the previous byte has not been read from **SPxDATA**. The bit is cleared when the register is read.

Transmit/Receive Summary

The following assumes that all of the other registers (**SPxDIV**, **SPxRPORT**, etc.) have already been setup as required.

Asynchronous Mode:

To transmit a byte all you need to do is write to the **SPxDATA** register

SPxSTAT:TxBufEmpty will be set when the byte transfers to the TSR. This will happen immediately for the first byte of a message.

SPxSTAT:TxBusy will be cleared when the transmitter is idle.

To receive a byte you need do nothing, **SPxSTAT:RxDone** will be set when a byte has been received.

Synchronous Mode:

Transmitting

Master Mode is the same as Asynchronous Mode

In Slave Mode you need to write to the **SPxDATA** register. The byte will not actually transmit, but will be placed into the TSR (if/when it is empty), until the Master requests it by supplying the clock signal. The **SPxSTAT** bits are affected the same as Asynchronous Mode.

Receiving

In Master Mode you need to set the **SPxRPORT:StartRx** bit to start the byte.

Slave Mode is the same as Asynchronous Mode.

Timers and Counters

This processor has sixteen timers: 0 – F. This is because timers are required for the eight Pulse Modulators. This leaves at least eight Timers for other uses.

Here are several uses for timer/counters which are based on the CPU clock:

- Clock source for Pulse Modulators
- Generate periodic interrupts
- Started and/or stopped via external signals to measure time interval. This is sometimes referred to as Input Capture
- Change the state of an output periodically based on the timer value (PWM and PPM)

In general, the terms timer and counter will be used interchangeably.

Since the logic used to create a timer is basically the same as a counter, it is quite easy to have a "Timer" use an external signal for its clock input instead of the CPU clock. The same device can be used to simply count input pulses from an external source.

The timer/counters used in this processor are 32 bit, synchronous, up-counters and will count up to their full value unless a count value has been programmed and enabled. When the counter reaches its maximum value the next clock will cause it to "wrap around" to a count of 0 and start over. There is an option to generate an interrupt when the count transitions from maximum to 0.

Timer/Counter Registers

TxDATA – (4 bytes, R/W, 0) Timer **x** Data Register

Reading this register will return the count value of the timer. In order to ensure there are no "stale" data problems the count value is latched into a holding register when the read request is initiated.

Writing to this register sets the maximum count value – if this feature is enabled via **TxCFG:6**. This has the effect of setting the frequency at which the counter will overflow. Since the total number of states includes 0 and N, the period is N+1 counts.

- Reset Value: 0x00000000

TxCLK – (1 byte, R/W, 0) Timer **x** Clock Source

Fig. 5.12

Bit(s)	7	6, 5, 4	3, 2, 1, 0
Internal Clock	0	000 = CPU 001 = PM y 010 = Tmr y	PM y or Tmr y
External Clock	1	Parallel Port	Bit nbr

Reset Value: 0x00

Internal Clock

Bit 7 = 0

Bits 6,5,4

000 = use CPU clock
001 = use output of Pulse Modulator y

This feature is used to count PM pulses. It can be used to turn them off after a specified number of pulses.

010 = use the pulses from Timer y overflow

This feature is used to cascade timers.

Bits 3,2,1,0 = Pulse Modulator or Timer Number

External Clock

Bit 7 = 1

Bits 6,5,4 = Parallel port which has the clock

Bits 2,1,0 = Bit of the parallel port which has the clock

If an external clock is used its frequency must be less than CPUclock/4 in order to allow synchronization with internal logic.

TxCFG – (1 byte, R/W, 0) Timer x Configure Register

Fig. 5.13

Bit(s)	7	6	5, 4	3	2, 1, 0
	State		*Mode*		
	0 = Disabled	0 = Full Count	00 = Free Run	1 = Clear Counter	Clock Prescale
	1 = Enabled	1 = Use Divisor	01 = Use TxStart & TxStop		
			10 = Stop on Overflow		
			11 = Enable while Timer y running		

Reset Value: 0x00

State: 1 = Enabled, 0 = Disabled

The Timer will run only if this bit is set. Depending on the configuration, this may not be the only condition required for the timer to run. This bit may be used to start and/or stop the timer via software. The design is such that the counter will not increment when this bit is changed.
This bit will get cleared to 0 when a Stop condition is detected (Modes 1-3)

Divisor: 0 = Use the full 32 bit count, 1 = use the divisor value written to **TxDATA**

Mode: Select the operating mode of the Timer.

00 = Free Run – The timer will run as long as bit 7 is set.

01 = Use the Start and Stop registers to determine when the timer runs.

10 = Stop the counter when it overflows.

11 = Enable while Timer Y is running – see TxSTOP

This feature allows one timer to be used as a gate for another.

Clear: 1 = Clear the counter data register

This signal will not cause an interrupt. The bit does not have to be reset.

Clock Prescale: Divide the selected clock by N+1 before being applied to the Timer input.

Here are two sample Configuration Register values using hexadecimal and binary:

Enable the counter, full count, clear counter, use the CPU Clock/6

= 0x80 + 0x08 + 0x06 = 0x8E

= 0b10001110

Enable the counter, use TxDATA for max count value, stop on overflow, clear counter

= 0x80 + 0x40 + 0x20 + 0x08 = 0xE8

= 0b11100100

TxSTART – (1 byte, R/W, 0) Timer **x** Start Select Register

Fig. 5.14

Bit(s)	7	6, 5, 4	3	2, 1, 0
	+ Edge	Parallel Port	– Edge	Bit nbr

Reset Value: 0x00

+ Edge: Enable the rising edge of the selected port/bit to start the Timer

Parallel Port: Select the parallel port for the start signal

– Edge: Enable the falling edge of the selected port/bit to start the Timer

Bit Nbr: Select the bit within the selected parallel port for the start signal

Note that the start can be triggered on either or both edges of the selected signal.

TxSTOP – (1 byte, R/W, 0) Timer x Stop Select Register

Fig. 5.15

Bit(s)	7	6, 5, 4	3	2, 1, 0
	+ Edge	Parallel Port	– Edge	Bit nbr
			Timer y	

Reset Value: 0x00

+ Edge: Enable the rising edge of the selected port/bit to stop the Timer

Parallel Port: Select the parallel port for the stop signal

– Edge: Enable the falling edge of the selected port/bit to stop the Timer

Bit Nbr: Select the bit within the selected parallel port for the stop signal.

Timer Y: Stop the counter when Timer Y overflows.
See **TxCFG:Mode** = 11

Note that the stop can be triggered on either or both edges of the selected signal. The stop signal will be ignored until one full clock cycle after the start has occurred. This allows the timer to start and stop on the same edge of the same signal.

TxINT – (1 byte, R/W, 0) Timer **x** Interrupt Register

Fig. 5.16

Bit(s)	7	6	5	4	3	2, 1, 0
	Overflow	Start	Stop			IPL

Reset Value: 0x00

Overflow: 1 = Enable an interrupt when the Timer overflows to a count of 0

Start: 1 = Enable an interrupt when the Start signal is applied

Stop: 1 = Enable an interrupt when the Stop signal is applied

IPL: Set the Interrupt Priority Level. 0 = interrupts disabled

The interrupt vector names for the Timers are **VECTOR_TMRx** where the "x" is replaced by the Timer number.

TxSTAT – (1 byte, R, 0) Timer **x** Status Register

Fig. 5.17

Bit(s)	7	6	5	4	3	2, 1, 0
	Overflow	Start	Stop		Running	

Reset Value: 0x00

Overflow: 1 = The Timer has overflowed

Start: 1 = A Start event has occurred

Stop: 1 = A Stop event has occurred

Running: 1 = Counter/Timer is running

Reading this register will clear the interrupt condition(s) and their associated bits. If multiple interrupt conditions are enabled, the ISR must be written so that it can handle any combination of them.

For those of you who are more hardware oriented, the following block diagram might be helpful. Most signals are from the registers. The underlined signals are generated within the processor:

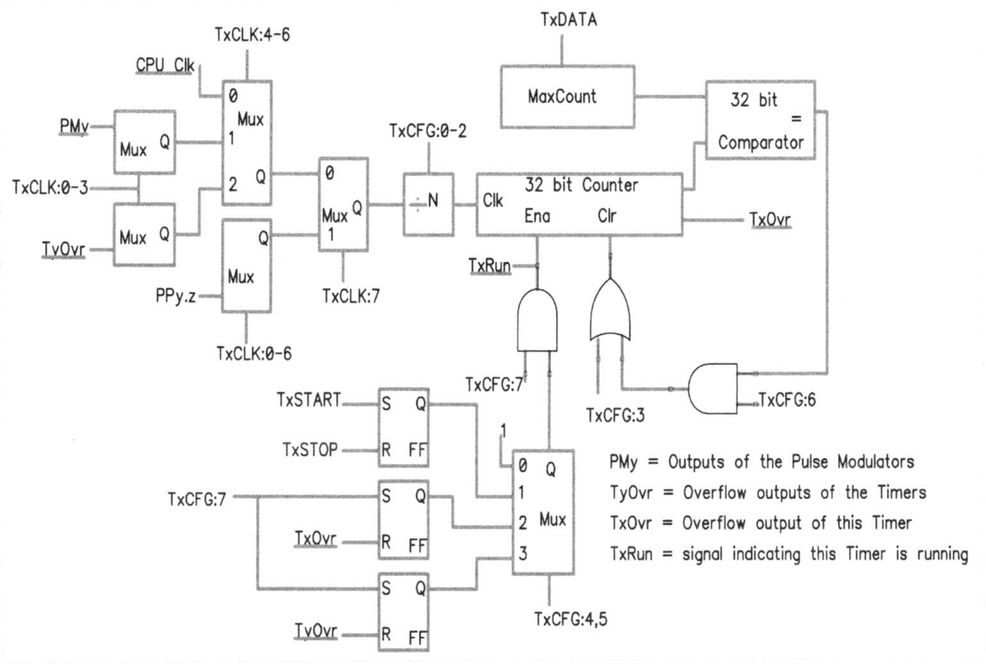

Fig. 5.18

Pulse Modulators

There are eight Pulse Modulators in this processor.

Most microprocessors have Pulse Width Modulators (PWM) and/or Pulse Position Modulators (PPM). These devices enable you to generate a continuous stream of pulses which vary in pulse width and/or position relative to a known "0" point. The method of setting up these devices in this processor is somewhat different than other systems I have used.

This system uses the previously described timers as the main driving device along with the counters described below.

The Pulse Modulation counters here are count down devices and stop when they reach 0. The output port and pin are selected via the appropriate **PPx.yCFG** register.

Pulse Modulator Registers

PMxCFG – (1 byte, R/W, 0) Pulse Modulator **x** Configuration Register

Fig. 5.19

Bit(s)	7	6, 5, 4	3	2, 1, 0
	Mode		*Edge*	
	0 = PPM	Timer nbr	0 = Start	IPL
	1 = PWM		1 = End	

Reset Value: 0

Mode: Select between PPM and PWM

Timer: The timer (0...7) to use for the Pulse Modulator.
Setting the TxDATA register will control the frequency of the Pulses

Edge: If interrupts are enabled, this selects which edge of the output pulse is used to generate the interrupt.

0 = leading/rising edge

1 = trailing/fallng edge

IPL: Set the Interrupt Priority Level. 0 = interrupts disabled.

The interrupt vector names for the Pulse Modulator are **VECTOR_PMx** where the "**x**" is replaced by the Pulse Modulator number.

PMxWIDTH – (4 bytes, R/W, 0) Pulse Modulator **x** Width Register

This register contains the number of timer pulses for which the output will be on. The counter will be loaded from the Width Register and start counting down when either the selected timer reaches 0 (**PMxCFG:7** = 1) or when the Delay Counter reaches 0 (**PMxCFG:7** = 0). The Width Counter will stop when it counts down to 0. While it is counting, the selected Parallel Port/Pin(s) will be at a logic '1".

PMxDELAY – (4 bytes, R/W, 0) Pulse Modulator **x** Delay Register

If PPM is selected, this will be the number of Timer pulses between a Timer count of 0 and when the pulse starts. The counter will be loaded from the Delay Register and start counting down when the selected Timer reaches 0.

Summary:

For both PWM and PPM:

The frequency is determined by the value written to **TxDATA** of the selected Timer and the clock signal driving the Timer.

The pulse terminates when the Width Counter counts down from the value written to the **PMxWIDTH** register.

The Width Counter stops counting when it reaches 0.

The diagram of Figure 5.20 shows a PWM signal.

The output pulse and the Width Counter start when the selected Timer transitions from its maximum count value to 0.

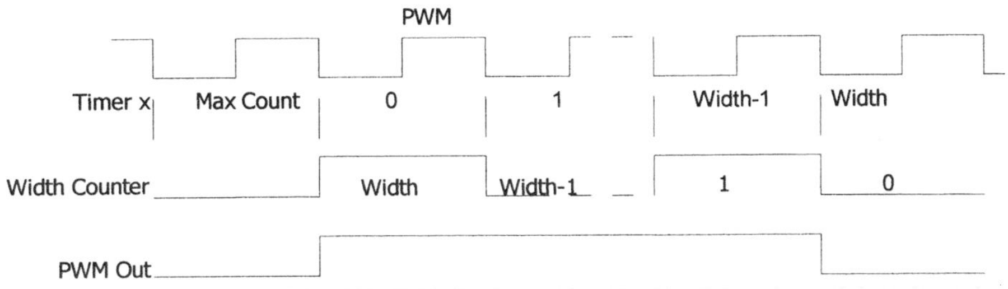

Fig. 5.20

The diagram of Figure 5.21 shows a PPM signal.

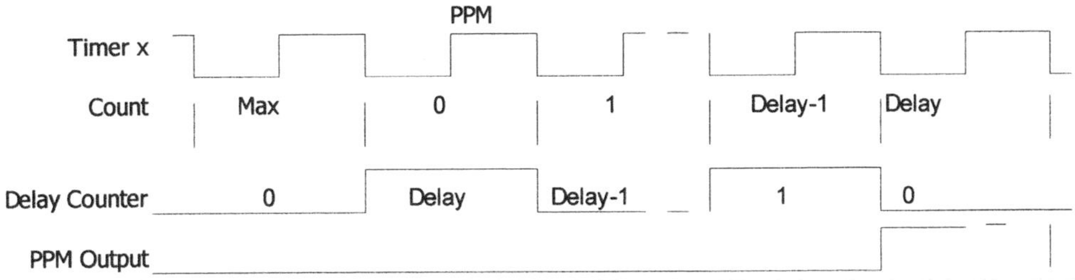

Fig. 5.21

- The Delay Counter starts when the Timer transitions from its maximum count value to 0.
- The Width Counter and the output pulse start when the Delay Counter counts down to 0.

The Delay Counter stops counting at this point.

Sample Port Assignments

The following table shows one possible allocation of I/O functions for the parallel ports. (See the **PPx.yCFG** register description.) All parallel ports have the same features for functions 0 – 2. For now, we will also say that all ports also have the same features for functions 4 – 7. This leaves function 3 as not defined.

Fig. 5.22

Function → PPx:Bit ↓	4	5	6	7
0	SP0Tx	SP4Tx	Clock 0	PM0
1			Clock 1	PM1
2	SP1Tx	SP5Tx	Clock 2	PM2
3			Clock 3	PM3
4	SP2Tx	SP6Tx	Clock 4	PM4
5			Clock 5	PM5
6	SP3Tx	SP7Tx	Clock 6	PM6
7			Clock 7	PM7

At first glance this may seem somewhat limiting. However, note that all of the I/O defined for this processor are available on EVERY port. This allows every Serial Port and every Pulse Modulator to be used and still have plenty of parallel I/O bits available. For instance:

- PP0 = Serial Ports 0 – 3 (the odd bits will be the receivers)
- PP1 = Serial Ports 4 – 7 (the odd bits will be the receivers)
- PP2 = clocks for all SPI serial ports
- PP3 = all Pulse Modulator outputs
- PP4 – PP7 = parallel I/O

Even if there would be more internal I/O devices, they could be made available on PP4 – PP7. Also, there is no “rule” that says that all internal I/O devices must be available on every port.

It is highly unlikely that a real processor would be designed this way, mainly due to the complexity of the switching required. Some processors will have the various I/O features on more than one parallel port, but there are those that make certain features available on only one specific port and bit.

When designing a microprocessor system it is extremely important to decide which features of the processor are required for your application and then to decide, if allowed, what port to use for each one. More than one designer has made incorrect assumptions about the availability of resources and has had to redesign a circuit board.

Other Features

- There is a second oscillator for a Real Time Clock. Its frequency is 32768Hz. It drives a 15 bit counter which generates an interrupt once per second. This one second signal also drives a 32 bit counter which can be used to determine date and time. The interrupt vector is **VECTOR_RTC**. There should be more registers associated with the RTC but, for purposes of this book they are not needed. Also, there would be a pin on the processor for a battery so that the RTC circuit would stay active even when main power is removed.

- This processor register has the frequency, in Hz, at which the processor is running: **CPU_FREQUENCY**.

- The PSR contains bits which describe how the program started. See *This Processor – Processor Status Register*.

External I/O

External I/O is a method of expanding the I/O capability of the processor with devices that are external to the microprocessor. Some early examples are:

- 8255 – Peripheral Parallel Interface. This was originally designed for the 8085 microprocessor and gave it three additional 8 bit parallel ports. It can easily be used by other processors.

- 6820 – Peripheral Interface Adapter. This is essentially Motorola's equivalent to the 8255, although it has fewer I/O.

- 6850 – Asynchronous Communications Interface Adapter. Also a Motorola device, this is a serial interface IC.

Any microprocessor system can be designed to access external I/O devices using the memory bus. This can be done relatively easily by using some of the upper address bits to enable a decoder which would then use lower address bits to generate chip select signals. One possibility is shown in Figure 5.23 (next page).

This is the scheme used by the PDP 11 – the upper address bits, when all on (or 1), were used to enable the I/O devices while the lower 13 bits were used to select among the I/O devices as well as to access their registers.

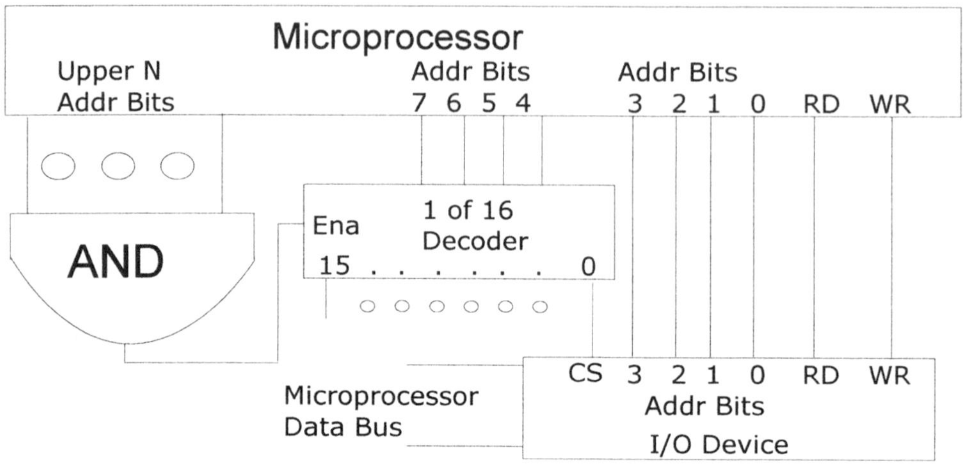

Fig. 5.23

Although this diagram shows only a single I/O device, there is provision for up to 16. All devices would share the signals coming directly from the microprocessor. Only the CS (Chip Select) signals need to be unique among the devices. Since I/O devices may be slower than memory, there should be a provision in the processor to add extra clock cycles to the control signals when the I/O devices are accessed. You will need to account for parameters such as:

- Setup time
- Hold time
- Minimum pulse widths
- Time between chip select and the RD and WR signals

An interesting feature to note is that if the RD and WR signals are the same as are used by the memory devices, then this External I/O method is Memory Mapped – it occupies the same address space as the memory. If the RD and WR signals are specifically for External I/O (separate from the memory signals) then this connection mechanism is not Memory Mapped and there would be special instructions to access the I/O. If they are separate, the signals will have different names such as IORD and IOWR.

If your system does use the memory signals for its external I/O, it is strongly recommended that you isolate the I/O devices using bus drivers and transceivers. These devices should be placed as close to the processor as possible in order to reduce bus loading capacitance. If this is not done, you run the risk of the I/O devices placing enough extra loading on the bus signals that accessing memory becomes a problem.

6
Assembler

The assembler and all the samples are available from my website *www.qsl.net\K3PTO* or you can email me at *K3PTO@ARRL.NET*. There is a screen shot of the assembler at the end of this chapter.

The job of the Assembler is to convert source code files into the binary codes that the processor can execute. It uses directives (described later in this chapter) in the files to determine the addresses of the instructions and data that have been entered into the files. The file created by the Assembler is often referred to as an "object" file and has a file type of '.obj'. **The features described in the following sections of this chapter are specific to the assembler that comes with this text.** Although most of them are specific to this assembler all assemblers will have similar features as well as restrictions on those features.

This assembler supports two instruction sets – see Chapters 8 and 13. When you run the assembler you can select which one you want to use. The symbol INSTRUCTION_SET will be set to either one or two based on your selection.

There is also an initialization file which is read when the assembler first starts and is updated when you exit. This file contains the following information:

- The name of the last file selected for assembly
- The path of the last file selected for assembly
- The instruction set number

These values will populate the appropriate controls upon being read. This is a text file and must be in the same folder as the assembler.

Now for some more definitions:

Value

A numeric constant

- Symbol

A meaningful name given to a numeric value. The rules for creating a symbol are:

- Any combination of:
  - Letters (upper and lower case) – case sensitive
  - Digits
  - Underscore
  - Period
- Must NOT start with a digit
- NO OTHER CHARACTERS ALLOWED
- Must be at least two characters and no longer than 16 characters – characters beyond 16 will be ignored. The 16 character limit is a limit of this assembler. Most assemblers allow at least 32.
- This assembler currently allows a maximum of 2000 symbols – including those found in Processor_Definitions.h (about 340).

Symbols will usually be created using the #define directive.

A good convention to follow is to use all upper case letters for symbol names (except those that are labels). This makes them easier to differentiate from labels.

- Label

A label is a special case of a symbol that refers to a memory address. The main difference between a label and a general symbol is that the label must be terminated with a colon where it is defined.

Labels are always used to identify memory locations such as:

- The starting address of a function or subroutine
- Addresses within a function or subroutine
- Variables
- Constants and Tables of constants

Expression

A combination of values, operators and symbols that reduces to a value. The simplest form of an expression is a value. All symbols used in an expression must be defined somewhere in the program.

Global

The property of a symbol that makes it known to the entire program. A global that resides in one assembly unit may be referenced by a function or expression in another. The Linker (see definition below) will insure that the instructions referencing the global get the correct address/value. Items in an assembly unit which need to be global, must be defined as such by an Assembler Directive. This assembler does not support Global references. Some assemblers use special notation for global labels – a double colon. This enables the programmer to define a label as global without using another assembler directive.

Linker

The job of a Linker is to take the binary files that have been created by the Assembler (and/or Compiler) and combine them into a single unit for programming the microprocessor. This is necessary because there may be references among the files that the Assembler does not know how to resolve. For instance: a function in one file may be called from another. For some systems a Linker is not needed, as will be the case when all files are assembled at one time.

For the purposes of this book, in order to simplify the assembler requirements, the entire program is assembled at one time – a single assembly unit. The usage of multiple files, assembled separately, requiring linking, is an added complexity that is not really required to learn Assembly Language.

Local

The property of a symbol that makes it known only to the assembly unit or function in which it is defined. Items which are not defined as global are automatically local.

Some more rules for this assembler:

Comments are preceded by a ";" (semi-colon). All characters on the line from the ";" and following are ignored.

C-style block comments are also valid (/*...*/). The only restriction is that block comments must be entire lines.

- White-space is collapsed to a single space except:
  - At the beginning and end of a line where it is removed
  - Within a string literal
- The default radix is 10
- The default radix can be overridden as follows:
  - Hexadecimal values can be noted using a 0x or 0X prefix
  - Binary values can be noted using a 0b or 0B prefix
  - Octal values can be noted using a 0o or 0O prefix
  - Decimal values can be noted using a 0d or 0D prefix
  - Floating Point values can be noted using a 0f or 0F prefix
    - Scientific notation may also be used: 1.234E–6
    - The decision to use single or double precision will be determined by usage
- A symbol must evaluate to a numeric value or a string literal of up to 8 bytes

Special Address Symbols

Note: there are several examples in this chapter which demonstrate all the features discussed here.

As you write your program there will be times when you need to force the assembler to use specific addresses. You will need to do this at least once at the beginning of your program in order to tell the assembler where ROM and RAM start. You may also want to specify an area for constants to be stored.

Most assemblers have a mechanism for defining a number of known symbols for doing exactly this. *These must be defined at the start of your program* and may be referenced throughout the program. In general you will not want to change them but you may if necessary. The ones used by this assembler are:

- NEXT_RAM – The address of the next value to be stored in RAM. As you insert variables the Assembler updates the value.

NEXT_ROM – The address of the next value to be stored in ROM. As you insert constants the Assembler updates the value.

NEXT_PC – The address of the next instruction. As you insert instructions the Assembler updates the value. There is a direct correlation between NEXT_PC and the microprocessor's PC when it is executing instructions. The assembler remembers the first value to which NEXT_PC is defined and will compare it to the value of NEXT_ROM each time NEXT_ROM is used. If NEXT_ROM ever reaches the initial value of NEXT_PC, an error will be generated.

Each of these symbols is defined and referenced using the #address directive (see definition in section *Setting Memory Addresses*).

Note: NEXT_ROM and NEXT_PC could be used interchangeably but it is not a good idea. Using them as defined keeps the program cleaner and easier to read. The only exception might be if the programmer wants to store some constants in the same memory area as the function which uses them. In this case, NEXT_PC should be used.

The term "Address Pointer" will be used to refer to the address which the assembler is currently using. The last symbol used of the three defined above is considered to be the Address Pointer and is automatically updated by the assembler. There is a short sample program later in this chapter which demonstrates the usage of these symbols and the directives which follow.

For a program that is going to be Assembly Language only, these address symbols are probably the only ones necessary. However, a program that is also going to include a higher level language will have a more complex set of symbols and directives used to set memory addresses.

An important feature of this assembler is that this assembler reads through the entire source file(s) twice:

Pass 1

Store the names of all symbols

Calculate the amount of memory required by each directive and instruction

Evaluate the Address Pointer values as the source files are read

Store the name of each label and its address

Pass 2

- Evaluate all symbols as they are encountered. An expression can use symbols even if they occur after the expression.

- Create the program list file. The list file is created in the same folder and has the same name as the file you are assembling but with a .LST file type.

- If this was a real processor, the binary file needed to program the processor execution memory would also be created

As the assembler processes the files, there will be times when it detects error and warning conditions. The difference between the two is that an error can cause the assembler to incorrectly calculate the address pointer value whereas a warning will use a default value to "correct" the condition. During assembler pass two the errors and warnings will be displayed in the text window of the assembler GUI as well as inserted into the list file.

Directives

Assembler Directives are used to give the Assembler some instructions that affect different aspects of the program. Among them are:

- Setting memory addresses
- Declaring storage for variables and constants
- Setting interrupt vectors
- Defining constants
- Conditional assembly instructions

The directives defined here are for the purposes of the examples used in this book. Similar directives will exist in any assembler, probably with different syntax. Some of the syntax used here will look like directives used in C.

General Directives

```
#define    <symbol> <expression>
```

There are many times in a program where the programmer should use a symbol for an expression instead of the expression itself. This is simply good programming practice. Here are some reasons why this should be done:

- Documentation – using a symbol makes the program more self-documenting. It also makes the program easier to read.

- Ease of maintenance – if an expression is used more than once in a program, using a symbol makes it easier to update since all that needs to be done is to change the definition one time and then assemble the program again.

The first parameter is the name to be given to the expression of the second parameter. If the second parameter is left blank, the assembler will default the value to one. All symbols will be stored as 64 bit values within the assembler.

Example: `#define PROGRAM_START 0x1000`

Anywhere the symbol PROGRAM_START is used in the program the assembler will replace it with the value 0x1000.

An expression may contain any combination of symbols, values and the following arithmetic and logical operators:

+	add
–	subtract or 2's-complement
*	multiply
/	divide
~	1's-complement (invert all the bits)
|	logical-or of the two values
&	logical-and of the two values
^	logical-exclusive-or of the two values

The expression is evaluated from left to right. Parentheses are not allowed – this assembler does not understand the concept of "operator precedence" or parentheses. Any symbol used in the expression must be defined somewhere in the program.

Caution: Be careful when using either **&** *or* **|** *(arithmetic operators) that you do not confuse them with* **&&** *or* **||** *(conditional operators).*

If a symbol that has not been #define'd, or is not a label, is used in an expression the assembler will generate a warning. The assembler listing will show the value of the expression, preceded with an equals sign, on the line where it is #define'd.

Another feature of some assemblers (and compilers as well) is that of allowing symbol names to be calculated. This is a very powerful feature and can be quite useful but really has nothing to do with programming in Assembly Language. It is even possible to create a programming language using this facility.

```
#global   <symbol name>
```

This directive defines the symbol in one of two ways:

- The symbol is to be found in another file and will be resolved by the linker.
- The symbol is in this file and is to be made available to other files via the linker.

Global values are not supported by this assembler and will not be used in the examples in this book.

```
#include   <file name>
```

There may be times when the programmer wants to use the content of another file that has some common definitions and/or functions in it. This directive enables that facility and operates similarly to the C directive. It allows the programmer to insert the entire contents of another file just as if it were typed into the program at the point where the #include is used.

Example: `#include   My_definitions.h`

Insert the contents of the file My_definitions.h at this point in the program.

This assembler uses the file "Processor_Definitions.h" to define all the internal registers and vector addresses. This file is automatically #include'd by the assembler and must be in the same folder as the assembler. Your source files can be anywhere, but the assembler will set the default folder to be the same as your main program.

```
#radix   <radix>   ; The radix value must be a constant.
```

This allows the programmer to set the default radix for all integer values which follow. The allowed values are: 2, 8, 10 and 16. The default for the assembler is 10. If you want to disable a default radix you must omit the radix value.

Example: `#radix   10`

```
#error   "text of message"
```

Allows the programmer to create an error based on a condition probably detected by comparing two expressions. See Conditional Assembly Directives later in this chapter.

Example:

```
#if NEXT_ROM >= NEXT_PC
   #error "NEXT_ROM incursion into NEXT_PC"
#endif
```

```
#warning "text of message"
```

Allows the programmer to print a warning message. Note: both #error and #warning are usually used within a conditional assembly block.

```
#print<value>     ; value must
#nprint<value>    ; be a constant
```

Allows the user to enable and/or disable printing sections of the assembly list file. The header file has a #print 0 as its first line and a #print PR_ALL as its last line. This inhibits printing all of the #define's in the file. These are the current symbols you may use to qualify what gets printed:

PR_ALL	enables printing of everything; this is the default value
PR_SYMBOL	allows you to disable printing of the entire Symbol Table
PR_PROC_DEFS	allows you to disable printing of the standard Processor Definitions in the Symbol Table. This is a subset of PR_SYMBOL
PR_UN_IF	allows you to disable printing of unsatisfied conditional assembly blocks

You may also use a value of 0 to disable all printing.

Here are a two examples:

```
#print     PR_ALL                      ; this is default value
#nprint    PR_PROC_DEFS | PR_UN_IF     ; disable printing the
                                       ; standard processor
                                       ; definitions and the
                                       ; unsatisfied conditional
                                       ; blocks
```

There is no real need for #nprint since it is possible to accomplish the same results using only #print. However, it is simpler and easier to formulate the correct value using #nprint if you want to disable printing a specific feature. For instance, the following two directives will usually have the same effect:

```
#nprint    PR_PROC_DEFS
#print     PR_ALL & ~PR_PROC_DEFS
```

The main difference in how the assembler handles these two directives is that #print loads the expression into its internal print flag variable whereas #nprint clears the specified bits in the print flag variable.

The implementation in this assembler is quite simplistic. Another assembler I used extensively had a separate counter for each possible print option. Each #print would increment the counter and #nprint would decrement it. The assembler would only print the portions of code for which its associated print counter was greater than 0.

```
#width   <number of columns>, <tab spacing>
```

This directive allows you to set the maximum number of columns as well as the tab spacing the assembler will use when printing the .LST file. The default values are 130 and 3, respectively.

Setting Memory Addresses

```
#address   <Address Symbol> (<expression>)
```

There are many times when the programmer wants to set either an absolute or a relative address. This directive causes the assembler to set the Address Symbol and the Address Pointer to the value of the expression.

If <expression> is omitted then the Address Pointer is simply set to the value of the specified Address Symbol. The expression must follow the same rules as those for #define.

Example: `#address   NEXT_PC`

Set the Address Pointer to the current value of NEXT_PC.

```
#address   NEXT_PC<expression>
```

Set both the Address Pointer and NEXT_PC to the value of the <expression>.

The only valid Address symbols are:

- NEXT_PC
- NEXT_ROM
- NEXT_RAM

```
#align  <alignment value> ; The argument must be a constant
```

Another instance of an incremental change is if there is a need to ensure that some data value or values be aligned to a specific memory boundary. The <alignment value> can be any of: 1, 2, 4, 8 or 16. One reason for using this directive is if the processor accesses memory more efficiently when the data it has to access is aligned on a specific boundary.

Example: `#align   4`

This causes the assembler to advance its Address Pointer (if necessary) such that it is evenly divisible by four. If it is already evenly divisible by the alignment value then no change is made.

There is an implied #align 2 whenever the #address directive references NEXT_PC. This is to ensure that all instructions start on an even byte boundary. The alignment value of 1 is a special case that forces the current Address Pointer to an odd value. This should be used only with NEXT_RAM or NEXT_ROM.

```
#vector    <interrupt vector address>
```

There must be a mechanism to tell the assembler the address of each ISR. The parameter tells the assembler which vector is being defined. (See *I/O Devices: Interrupts*)

The <interrupt vector address> is defined by the processor architecture since the processor will have a specific address for each interrupting device and is usually a predefined symbol known to the assembler. All of the interrupt vector addresses are defined in Processor_Definitions.h.

The assembler will use the value of NEXT_PC as the address of the ISR. This allows (maybe "forces" would be more accurate) the programmer to insert the directive immediately preceding the declaration of the ISR.

For this assembler all of the interrupt vector addresses are defined as follows:

```
VECTOR_<unique name for the device>    ; See the chapter on I/O
                                       ; Devices
```

Using the pre-defined names allows the programmer to use the #vector directive without having to know the actual <interrupt vector address> values.

```
Example:        #vector  VECTOR_START   ; use the value of NEXT_PC as
                                        ; the startup address

Example:        #vector  VECTOR_SPOTX   ; use the value of NEXT_PC as
                                        ; the Serial Port 0
                                        ; Transmit ISR
```

The #vector does not affect the Address Pointer. It causes the assembler to insert the ISR address at the specified location in the memory image (the <interrupt vector address>) it creates during the assembly process. These could also be defined using the #address directive and just listing the ISR addresses. However, that method forces the programmer to insert the <address of ISR> values in the proper order, starting at address 0, and have no missing entries.

IMPORTANT: any interrupt vector that does not have an ISR will automatically get the VECTOR_ERROR value. This is an ISR that will be executed if an undefined/unexpected interrupt occurs. This means that the programmer should implement the VECTOR_ERROR

ISR. If the programmer does not implement this ISR the assembler will insert a dummy ISR that will cause the program to start over.

There are two vectors that must be defined in your program or the assembler will generate an error:

VECTOR_START – defines the starting address of the program

VECTOR_RTC – defines the address of the ISR for the Real Time Clock

This was done in order to make you aware that there are a number of "things you must do" in every assembly language program. You will need to become very familiar with the requirements of your microprocessor and the assembler you are using.

Declaring Storage for Variables and Constants

Every program uses variables and constants. In higher level languages all you need to do is to declare them in any of several ways depending on how you are going to use them. The compiler (or interpreter) will decide where to put them in memory based on several criteria, among which are: do they go on the stack or are they global? In C you can declare variables within your code. In Assembly Language it is not so easy. You have to not only declare your variables and constants, you must also place them in memory.

RAM is used as the location of values that will be modified during program execution. ROM is used for program code and constants. However, in many systems the program actually executes out of RAM. In these cases it is generally expected that these locations are treated as read-only. The processor can even have a hardware feature that disallows writing to these memory locations once the program has started.

```
#alloc
```

The #alloc directive allocates storage for one or more variables or constants with their sizes being defined by a suffix of a period followed by a digit 1, 2 ,4 or 8 as shown in the following examples.

Note: when the #alloc size is 2, 4 or 8, the Address Pointer will be forced to an even value by adding one if required.

This form of the directive is the one that will be used to define single element variables:

```
Value_1:    #alloc.1    ; create a 1 byte variable with the name
                        ; Value_1
Value_2:    #alloc.4    ; create a 4 byte variable with the name
                        ; Value_2
```

These forms of the directive allows the programmer to insert "named" constants and tables in memory.

```
Constant_1:        #alloc.2  0x1234       ; create a 2 byte value
Constant_Values:   #alloc.1  1,2,3,4,5    ; create a table of 5
                                          ; bytes
String_1:          #alloc.s  "string\0"   ; create a text string
                                          ; that is NULL
                                          ; terminated
```

This last version allows the programmer to create a string literal. There are several special character values that can be included in a string literal for formatting purposes:

\0	; insert a byte value of 0 – this is useful for terminating the string
\n	; ASCII line feed
\r	; ASCII carriage return character
\t	; ASCII tab character
\\	; ASCII back slash character
\"	; ASCII quote character

```
#allocb.n<number of elements>
```

This directive is similar to #alloc except that it allocates a block of memory with the number of elements specified as a parameter. This is the directive you would probably want to use for creating an array in RAM.

```
Block_1:  #allocb.1 10   ; allocate 10 elements of 1 byte each
Block_2:  #allocb.8 32   ; allocate 32 elements of 8 bytes each
```

The Address Pointer will be advanced by the appropriate amount after each directive is evaluated. The amount of memory you can allocate is limited only by the addressable space (32 bits) of the computer.

Note: when the #allocb size is 2, 4 or 8, the Address Pointer will be forced to an even value by adding one if required.

```
#def_data_size <0, 1, 2, 4, 8>  ; set the default data size.
                                ; The argument must be a
                                ; constant
```

This directive allows you to be "lazy" with the instructions. Instead of specifying the data size with most instructions, you can simply specify those that are different from the default value. If you do not use this directive, any instruction requiring a size specifier which does not have one, will be flagged with a warning and a default value of 2 will be used.

You can disable this feature by setting the parameter to 0. This is the default for this directive.

WARNING: if you are not careful, this feature can cause you to use an incorrect instruction which will probably be hard to spot!

Sample Program

```
; Sample_Alloc.asm

#nprint    PR_PROC_DEFS                ; do not print the
                                       ; processor definitions

; define the starting addresses for each of the known areas
; of memory
; remember that the first 0x400 bytes are for the interrupt
; vectors

#radix     10                          ; set the default radix
#address   NEXT_ROM  0x400             ; start storing constants
                                       ; at 0x400
#address   NEXT_PC   NEXT_ROM+0x1000   ; allow an area of 0x1000
                                       ; bytes for constants
#address   NEXT_RAM  0x30000           ; RAM starting address –
                                       ; sets the Address Pointer

Value_1:   #alloc.1                    ; create a 1 byte variable
                                       ; with the name Value_1
Value_2:   #alloc.4                    ; create a 4 byte variable
                                       ; with the name Value_2

; NEXT_RAM now is 0x30006 due to the #alloc.4 being forced to
; start on an even address

#address   NEXT_ROM                    ; set the Address Pointer
                                       ; to NEXT_ROM (0x400)
Const_1:   #alloc.2  0x1234            ; create a 2 byte constant
Const_Values:   #alloc.1  1,2,3,4,5    ; create a table of
                                       ; constants with 5 bytes

; NEXT_ROM now is 0x407

#address   NEXT_PC                     ; set the Address Pointer
                                       ; to NEXT_PC (0x1400)
```

```
#vector   VECTOR_START                 ; set startup vector to the
                                       ; value of NEXT_PC
Program_Start:                         ; label of the start of the
                                       ; program
#allocb.1 0x1234                       ; dummy directive to
                                       ; simulate block of code

; NEXT_PC is now 0x1400 + 0x1234 = 0x2634

; set up some variables for Function_1
#address  NEXT_RAM                     ; set the Address Pointer
                                       ; to NEXT_RAM (0x30006)
Block_1:  #allocb.1  10                ; allocate 10 elements of 1
                                       ; byte each
Block_2:  #allocb.8  32                ; allocate 32 elements of 8
                                       ; bytes each

; NEXT_RAM now is 0x30006 + 10. + (32 * 8) =
; 0x30006 + 0x000A + 0x0100 = 0x30110

#address  NEXT_PC                      ; set the Address Pointer
                                       ; to NEXT_PC (0x2634)
Function1_Consts:
#alloc.4  54321, 0x12345, 98765, 56789    ; some constants for
                                          ; Function_1

; NEXT_PC is now 0x2634 + 16. = 0x2644
Function_1:
#allocb.1 0x234                        ; dummy directive to
                                       ; simulate block of code

; NEXT_PC is now 0x2644 + 0x234. = 0x2878

; ISR for serial port one transmitter

#vector   VECTOR_SP1TX                 ; use NEXT_PC as the value
                                       ; for <address of ISR>
                                       ; SP1TxISR:

; code for the transmit ISR
```

Programming suggestions:

- Note that the various "fields" of text above seem to be aligned in columns. This is simply good programming technique. The program is much easier to read if programming elements are aligned in columns. But, please do not carry it to extremes! The line with the label "Function1_Consts" does not line up. There is no reason to make all the other lines of code line up with this one.

- Document your code as you write it! Thinking that you will come back to it later is a nice thought that is rarely carried out in practice.

Conditional Assembly Directives

There are many times when it is desirable to create programs that have several variations. The programmer will need a way to cause blocks of code to either be included or excluded during the assembly process. Conditional directives enable this feature. The conditional directives used in this assembler are very similar to their equivalent directive in C.

The following relational operators may be used when comparing values:

- = the expressions must be equal
- == same as =, allowed in order to maintain compatibility with C
- != the expressions must not be equal
- > the first expression must be greater than the second expression
- >= the first expression must be greater than or equal to the second expression
- < the first expression must be less than the second expression
- <= the first expression must be less than or equal to the second expression
- && both expressions must not be 0
- || either of the two expressions must not be 0

All symbols used in the conditional directive expressions must be capable of being evaluated during the first pass of the Assembler. This means that only symbols that have been previously defined can be used.

The rules for the expressions are identical to those for symbols – see the #define section.

Caution (repeated): Be careful when using either && or || (conditional operators) that you do not confuse them with & or | (arithmetic operators).

```
#if    <expression1> <relational operator> <expression2>
```

The condition is true if the expression evaluates to a non-zero value.

```
#if   VERSION = 1
```

The symbol VERSION must have been previously #define'd to the value 1 in order for the condition to be met.

```
#else
```

The block of code and/or directives following the #else will only be assembled if the associated #if has evaluated to false.

```
#endif
```

End the conditional assembly block started by the associated #if.

Assemblers usually allow the following two directives as well:

```
#ifdef (or #if defined) <expression>
```

The condition is true if the expression has been previously defined.

```
#ifndef (or #if !defined) <expression>
```

The condition is true if the expression has NOT been previously defined.

Two notes concerning #ifdef and #ifndef:

- This assembler supports only the shorter version of these last two conditional directives.
- Due to way this assembler handles these directives, there is a maximum of 100 allowed instances of them. This should be more than adequate for any practical program.

The assembler listing uses some special notation for #if blocks:

- Displayed on the line with the directive are
  - The nesting level and a true/false indication

example: 1:0	indicates level 1 with the condition not met
example: 2:1	indicates level 2 with the condition met

  - The value(s) of the expression(s)

- Statements within the block that do NOT get assembled due to the condition not being met are prefixed with a hyphen (as long as unsatisfied conditionals are being printed).

In general it is possible to have nested conditional blocks. However, it is recommended that nesting be kept to a minimum or it may get difficult to follow. It is also a good idea to use indentation when nesting in the same way that high level languages uses nesting. This assembler supports conditional nesting up to 10 levels. Attempting to use more than 10 levels will result in an error.

In this sample the label Startup_Message contains a string which gets assembled in one of two ways depending on whether or not the symbol DEBUGGING has been defined.

```
Startup_Message:

#alloc.s      "Code "
#ifdef        DEBUGGING                ; include the code block
                                       ; only if DEBUGGING has
                                       ; been #define'd
   #alloc.s   "NOT "
#endif

#alloc.s      "assembled for debugging\n\r\0"
```

This could just as easily have been coded as:

```
Startup_Message:

#ifdef        DEBUGGING                ; include the code block
                                       ; only if DEBUGGING has
                                       ; been #define'd
   #alloc.s   "Code assembled for debugging\n\r\0 "
#else
   #alloc.s   "Code NOT assembled for debugging\n\r\0 "
#endif
```

In either case the results are identical.

Sample Program

Here is a simple sample of nesting conditional directives. Note that the #endif has a comment indicating the expression used in the corresponding #if. Along with indenting, this is a good method of documenting which #if corresponds to the #endif.

```
#if          SYMBOL_1 = 1
   #if          SYMBOL_2 = 1
                ; here if SYMBOL_1 = 1 and SYMBOL_2 = 1
                ; some code and/or directives
   #else
                ; here if SYMBOL_1 = 1 and SYMBOL_2 != 1
                ; some code and/or directives
   #endif       ; SYMBOL_2 = 1
#else           ; SYMBOL_1 != 1
   #if       SYMBOL_2 = 1
                ; here if SYMBOL_1 != 1 and SYMBOL_2 = 1
                ; some code and/or directives
   #else
                ; here if SYMBOL_1 != 1 and SYMBOL_2 != 1
                ; some code and/or directives
   #endif       ; SYMBOL_2 = 1
#endif          ; SYMBOL_1 = 1

; Here is the same sample without using indenting or the
; additional comments:

#if          SYMBOL_1 = 1
#if          SYMBOL_2 = 1
                ; some code and/or directives
#else
                ; some code and/or directives
#endif
#else
#if          SYMBOL_2 = 1
                ; some code and/or directives
#else
                ; some code and/or directives
#endif
#endif
```

I hope you will agree that the first sample is easier to follow. The advantages of the methods used in the first sample will be more apparent when the nesting is more complex.

Reading the Assembler List File

Here is a sample source code file which was processed by the assembler. This is by no means a complete program. It is meant simply to demonstrate what the assembler does and how to interpret the assembler output.

```
;Test_ListFile.asm

#define     SYMBOL1    1              ; 1 byte
#define     SYMBOL2    0x1234         ; 2 byte
#define     SYMBOL4    0x123456       ; 4 byte
#define     SYMBOL8    0x1234567890   ; 8 byte

#address    NEXT_ROM   0x400

TextLabel: #alloc.s    "\tText with leading tab and ending LF,CR
                        and Null byte.\n\r\0"
Label1:     #alloc.1   10,20
#alloc.2    10,20,30
#alloc.4    10,20,30
#alloc.8    10,20,30

#address    NEXT_PC    0x1000
#vector     VECTOR_START
#vector     VECTOR_RTC

Main:
   copy.4   #Label1, R0               ; get the address of the
                                      ; bytes
   copy.1   (R0), R1                  ; get the 1st byte
```

In general it is a good idea to print assembler output using a non-proportional type font so that you can line up the various sections of the lines in columns.

The assembler output is shown in the same font as the listing above. A few notes about this list file:

- The font has been made smaller to help accommodate the paper width.
- Some of the lines from the assembler output are longer than can be displayed on one line of this paper size so they appear on the following line with the symbol “>” prefixed.
- This listing does not include the symbol table
- The explanatory text follows the assembler listing.

```
test_listfile.asm  07-03-2010  19:26:08

        ************** Interrupt Vectors **************

Vector     ISR Address
00000000   00001000
00000004   00001000

       ****************** Program ******************

 1:<path>\test_listfile.asm
 2:<path>\Processor_Definitions.h
 2:001 00000000                    #print  0      ; disable printing
 2:395 00000000                    #print  PR_ALL ; enable printing
 1:<path>\test_listfile.asm
 1:001 00000000                    ;Test_Listfile.asm
 1:002 00000000
 1:003 00000000 =01                #define SYMBOL1  1        ; 1-byte
 1:004 00000000 =1234              #define SYMBOL2  0x1234   ; 2-byte
 1:005 00000000 =00123456          #define SYMBOL4  0x123456 ; 4-byte
 1:006 00000000 =0000001234567890  #define SYMBOL8  0x1234567890  ; 8-
                                   >byte
 1:007 00000000
 1:008 00000400                    #address NEXT_ROM  0x400
 1:009 00000400
 1:010 00000400                    TextLabel: #alloc.s  "\tText with
                                   >leading tab and ending LF,CR and
                                   >Null byte.\n\r\0"
 1:010 00000400 09 54 65 78 74 20 77 69 74 68 20 6C 65 61 64 69 6E 67
                                   >20 74 61 62 20 61 6E 64 20 65 6E
                                   >64 69 6E 67 20 4C 46 2C 43
 1:010 00000426 52 20 61 6E 64 20 4E 75 6C 6C 20 62 79 74 65 2E 0A 0D
                                   >00
 1:011 00000439 0A 14              Label1:     #alloc.1  10,20
 1:012 0000043C 000A 0014 001E     #alloc.2     10,20,30
 1:013 00000442 0000000A 00000014  #alloc.4     10,20,30
 1:013 0000044A 0000001E
 1:014 0000044E 000000000000000A   #alloc.8     10,20,30
 1:014 00000456 0000000000000014
 1:014 0000045E 000000000000001E
 1:015 00000466
 1:016 00001000                    #address NEXT_PC       0x1000
 1:017 00001000                    #vector  VECTOR_START
 1:018 00001000                    #vector  VECTOR_RTC
```

```
1:019 00001000
1:020 00001000                        Main:
1:021 00001000 26C0 00000439          copy.4   #Label1, R0 ; get the
                                      >address of the bytes
1:022 00001006 0641                   copy.1   (R0), R1    ; get the 1st
                                      >byte

0 Errors    0 Warnings
```

First an important note: The assembler prints ALL values in hexadecimal independent of the radix of the values as entered in the source code. The only exceptions are floating point values in the Symbol Table which are displayed as double precision (64 bit) floating point.

The first section lists all the defined interrupt vectors with the interrupt vector address in the first column and the Interrupt Service Routine address in the second.

In general, each line of the listing for the "Program" section consists of the following:

- The file number
- A ":" separator
- The line number within the file
- The value of the current Address Pointer
- Values determined during assembly
  - Multiple values on a line are separated by one or more spaces
  - The printed Address Pointer is the address of the low byte of the first value
  - Each value is shown with its lowest byte as the right-most two hex digits
  - Successive values are stored in successively higher memory addresses
- Actual text of the source file starting in column 41
- The assembler will attempt to break long lines at the space character closest to and less than the maximum character position. These "extra" lines will be printed without the line number.

Line-by-line description of the above list file:

1:	The name and path of the main file being assembled
2:	The name and path of Processor_Definitions.h
2:001	Print directive disabling all print output
2:395	Enable printing
1:	Back to file number 1, the main program file, starting at line 1
1:001	Comment containing file name – good practice to have the file name on line 1
1:002	Blank line
1:003	Defines a 1 byte symbol. Note that the assembler prints the value of the symbol, preceded by an "=", based on its size.
1:004 – 1:006	More symbol definitions using larger values.
1:007	Blank line
1:008	Directive to set the address to the area of memory for constants in ROM. Note that the Address Pointer value is set to the value specified in the directive.
1:009	Blank line
1:010	abel and a text allocation directive. Note that there are no values shown on the line other than the Address Pointer. The following two lines, also starting with 1:010, have the byte values for each of the characters specified within the quotation marks. The assembler will only print up to 38 byte values on a line then print on the next line until done. Each line that is printed shows the starting address for that line of bytes.
1:011	Another label with a byte allocation directive of three bytes. Note that the Address Pointer is odd. This is because the previous directive was for an odd number of bytes. Note also that both byte values are printed on the same line as the source statement. If there are more bytes than can be printed in the allocated 40 character positions, any bytes that do not fit will be printed on subsequent lines. See lines 1:012 and 1:013.
1:012	Directive to store three word (2 byte) values. Note that the Address Pointer is an even number. The #alloc directive will force an even starting address for directives specifying 2, 4 or 8 byte values. If this were not the case the address of the first value would be 0x043B which is an odd number. Remember that the right-most two digits of a multi-byte value are the LSByte which is stored at the lowest address. In this case, for the value 0x000A – the LSByte is 0A and is stored at 0x043C while the MSByte is 0x00 and is stored at 0x043D. The address of the next 2 byte value (0x0014) is 0x043E which contains the low byte of 0x14. The upper byte of 0x00 is at address 0x043F.
1:013	Directive to store three longword (4 byte) values. In this case, only two values fit on the first line while the third is printed on the following line – still labeled as 1:014 but with the appropri-

	ate address indicated.
1:014	Directive to store three quadword (8 byte) values. In this case only one value fits per line.
1:015	Blank line
1:016	Set the Address Pointer to the value of NEXT_PC and defines NEXT_PC
1:017	Define "this" address as the Startup vector
1:018	Define "this" address as the Real Time clock vector – in this case, a dummy assignment to avoid an assembler error.
1:019	Blank line
1:020	label for the main program
1:021	A copy instruction with a data size of 4 bytes. The values printed are: • Address Pointer • Instruction Opcode (two bytes) • The value to be copied. In this case the value is the address of Label1 (see line 11).
1:022	Another copy instruction, this time with 1 byte data values. In this case there are no more values since both arguments are based only on register contents.

Following this section (not shown) will be the Symbol Tables in the following order:

- Labels
- 1, 2 and 4 byte values (if the value is negative, it will be prefixed with an "m")
- 8 byte values
- Floating point values
- Text values

These are printed with the value first followed by a single space and the symbol name. The number of items printed on a line are determined by the data size of the values (1, 2, 4 or 8 bytes) plus the 16 bytes required for the symbol names. The assembler limits the number of characters on a line to 132.

Assembler Screen Shot

As you can see from the picture, this is a very simple assembler. Here are the steps to follow:

1 Create your source file using your favorite text editor

2 Run the assembler (if not already running)

3 Open the file (if not already selected) using the "Open File" command

4 Select the appropriate Instruction Set

5 Press the "Run" command

You can leave your source file open, as long as you have saved it, when you run the assembler so that if there are any errors or warnings you can immediately switch to the source and edit it. If you also leave the assembler running, you can just press "Run" again to re-assemble the same file.

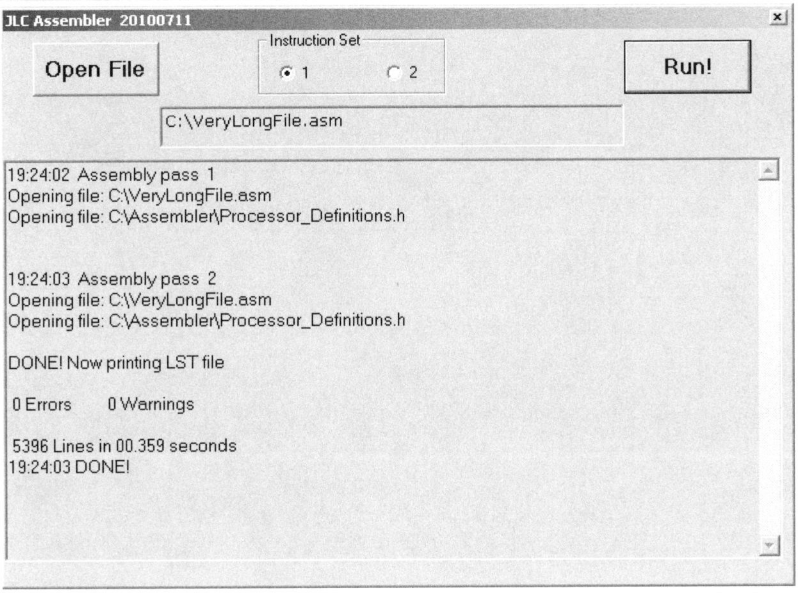

Fig. 6.1

7
Introduction to Instruction Sets

This chapter will introduce you to a few instruction sets. The following chapter describes in detail the instruction set for the "this processor". The processors used as examples in this section are: PDP11 and VAX, Rabbit, ARM and 68HC11. Here are some characteristics of each of the processors:

PDP11

- 16 bit processor
- Orthogonal Instruction Set
- One or two sets of eight general purpose registers
- CISC
- Some versions were microprogrammed

VAX

- 32 bit processor
- Orthogonal Instruction Set
- Sixteen 32 bit general purpose registers
- CISC

Rabbit

- 8 or16 bit processor depending on version
- NOT Orthogonal Instruction Set
- Number of registers depends on version but all have two sets of eight 8 bit registers and two index registers. Most 8 bit registers can be paired to form 16 bit registers
- CISC

ARM

- 32 or 16 (Thumb mode) bit processor
- Orthogonal Instruction Set

- 16 general purpose registers + more for floating point
- Listed as RISC (but has more instructions than PDP11) – instructions execute in a single cycle.

68HC11

- 8 bit processor
- NOT Orthogonal Instruction Set
- Two 8 bit Accumulators, two Index registers, SP and PC. The 8 bit accumulators can be paired to form a 16 bit accumulator.
- CISC

The Rabbit, ARM and 68HC11 are all considered as *Load and Store* processors – *most* arithmetic and logical instructions operate on register contents, there are several exceptions in each.

Values in memory which need to be accessed and operated on must be first read into a register and then written back to memory if required.

Instruction Categories

This is not meant to be an exhaustive listing of all possible categories of instructions but just a brief description that will introduce you to the concepts.

Double Operand

These instructions allow you to perform normal arithmetic operations such as: *add*, *subtract*, *multiply* and *divide*. There are also instructions that perform logical operations: or, and, exclusive-or and bit test. This category also includes instructions to copy data from one location to another.

Most assembly languages refer to the two operands as *source* and *destination*. In general the source operand is not modified while the destination receives the result of the operation. The order of the two operands is strictly assembler dependent.

The PDP11 and VAX instructions have the destination as the second operand while the 8080 and its derivatives have the destination as the first operand. The ARM instructions also have the destination as the first operand.

The examples for the 68HC11 show the destination as the first operand.

Here are a few examples:

PDP11 and VAX: (note: R0, R1 and R4 are 16 bit (PDP-11) or 32 bit (VAX) registers)

```
mov   #5, R0       ; move (copy) a value of 5 to R0
add   R0, R1       ; add the contents of R0 to the contents
                   ; of R1 and put the result into R1
sub   LOC1, R4     ; subtract the contents of LOC1 (location
                   ; in memory) from R4
sub   R4, LOC1     ; subtract the contents of R4 from the
                   ; contents of LOC1 and put the result in
                   ; LOC1
```

Rabbit processors: (note: A and B are 8 bit registers)

```
ld    A, 5         ; load (copy) a value of 5 into A
add   A, B         ; add the contents of B to the contents of
                   ; A and put the result into A
sub   B            ; subtract the contents of B from the
                   ; contents of A and put the result into A
```

This last instruction has an implied second operand of register A. There is no equivalent that will put the result into a memory location.

ARM: (note: R0, R1 and R2 are registers)

```
mov   R0, #5        ; copy a value of 5 to R0
add   R0, R1, R2    ; add R1 and R2, put the result into R0
```

68HC11:

```
ldaa  #5           ; load a value of 5 into the A accumulator
aba                ; add accumulators A and B, put the result
                   ; into A
sba                ; subtract accumulator B from A, put the
                   ; result into A
```

Note that none of these instructions explicitly show two operands but that there are implied operands for each of them.

Single Operand

These instructions essentially use a single operand as both source and destination. The operand is usually accessed using a read-modify-write sequence: the operand is first read, then modified and then written back to its original location. In some processors the operand can be modified in-place.

I tend to put even these instructions into two subcategories: arithmetic and shift/rotate. The arithmetic category includes instructions such as: increment, decrement, clear and complement. Most of these instructions can be implemented using specific double operand instructions – this is addressed in the chapter *A Few Algorithms*.
Here are a few examples of arithmetic instructions:

PDP11 and VAX:

```
inc   R0         ; add one to R0
dec   R1         ; subtract one from R1
clr   LOC1       ; set memory address LOC1 to 0
```

Rabbit processors:

```
inc   A          ; add one to register A
dec   B          ; subtract one from register B
xor   A          ; this is the most efficient way to clear
                 ; register A
```

ARM:

I have never programmed an ARM but as near as I can tell there are no instructions that are specifically single operand.

68HC11:

```
inca             ; add one to accumulator A
deca             ; subtract one from accumulator A
clrb             ; set accumulator B to 0
```

Here are some of the shift and rotate group:

Note: The difference between shift and rotate is described in the chapter "Instruction Set."

PDP11 and VAX:

```
asr   R0         ; arithmetic shift right R0 1 bit to the right
rol   R0         ; rotate register R0 1 bit to the left
```

Rabbit processors:

```
sra              ; arithmetic shift right register A 1 bit
                 ; to the right
rl    A          ; rotate register A 1 bit to the left
```

ARM:

Many ARM instructions can perform a shift or rotate as part of the instruction execution. Here is just one example:

```
sub   R4, R5, R7, LSR R2   ; logical shift right R7 by the
                           ; amount specified in R2, subtract
                           ; this result from R5 and place
                           ; the result into R4
```

68HC11:

```
asra                  ; arithmetic shift right accumulator A
                      ; 1 bit to the right
rolb                  ; rotate accumulator B 1 bit to the left
```

Program Counter

The Program Counter instructions enable the program to change the flow of instruction execution. Without this type of instruction, the program would simply execute instructions in sequence starting at address 0 and going up in memory until there is no more memory. There are two subcategories of these instructions: unconditional and conditional.

Some examples of unconditional program counter instructions:

PDP11 and VAX:

```
jmp   LOC1            ; jump to memory address LOC1
jsr   PC, LOC1        ; save Program Counter on the stack, jump
                      ; to the subroutine at LOC1
rts   (SP)+           ; return from subroutine. Retrieve PC from
                      ; stack
```

Rabbit processors:

```
jp    LOC1            ; jump to memory address LOC1
call  LOC1            ; save Program Counter on the stack, jump
                      ; to the subroutine at LOC1
ret                   ; return from subroutine. Retrieve PC from
                      ; stack
```

ARM:

```
b     LOC1            ; jump to memory address LOC1
```

```
bl     LOC1            ; save Program Counter in Link Register,
                       ; jump to the subroutine at LOC1
mov    PC, R14         ; return from subroutine called by bl
```

68HC11:

```
jmp    LOC1            ; jump to memory address LOC1
jsr    LOC1            ; save current Program Counter on the
                       ; stack, jump to the subroutine at LOC1
rts                    ; return from subroutine. Retrieve PC from
                       ; stack
```

Here a few of the conditional instructions:

PDP11 and VAX:

```
beq    LOC1            ; branch if equal to 0; branch to address
                       ; LOC1 if the Z-bit is set – the result of
                       ; the previous instruction resulted in a
                       ; value of 0
sob    R0, LOC1        ; subtract one from R0, branch to address
                       ; LOC1 if R0 does not equal 0. This
                       ; instruction is used to create counted
                       ; loops
```

Rabbit processors: (note: A and B are 8 bit registers)

```
jr     z, LOC1         ; jump to address LOC1 if the Z-bit is set
djnz   LOC1            ; subtract one from register B, branch to
                       ; address LOC1 if  B does not equal 0.
                       ; This instruction is used to create
                       ; counted loops
```

ARM:

```
cb     nz, R0, LOC1  ; branch to address LOC1 if R0 is not 0
```

68HC11:

```
beq    LOC1            ; branch if equal to 0; branch to address
                       ; LOC1 if the Z-bit is set
```

There is no equivalent to the sob or djnz in this instruction set.

Miscellaneous

There are always instructions that do not fit into a well defined category – unless that category has only one or two instructions. Here are a few.

PDP11 and VAX:

```
halt            ; stop executing instructions – usually a
                ; system reset is required to start the
                ; program again
wait            ; suspend execution until an interrupt
                ; occurs
```

Rabbit processors:

```
nop             ; no operation – essentially a time
                ; waster. This can be used effectively in
                ; tuning a loop so that it takes a
                ; specific number of clocks to execute
ccf             ; complement the carry flag – most useful
                ; after executing the scf which sets the
                ; carry flag
```

ARM:

```
clz   R0, R1    ; R0 = number of leading 0's in R1
adr   R0, LOC1  ; R0 = offset from PC to LOC1
```

68HC11:

```
nop             ; same as Rabbit
wai             ; wait for interrupt – same as PDP-11
```

8
Instruction Set

As you will see, the instruction set about to be defined in this chapter has less than 100 discrete instructions. However, most have a number of variations, some as many as 80! The variations are due to the operand sizes and addressing mode combinations that are allowed. Once you understand the operation of the basic instruction and the addressing modes, you will be able to use all those combinations – without having to refer to any documentation. Another important feature is that the instructions use the condition codes uniformly. In order to write a program all you need is a list of the basic instructions – you do not need to look up what each variation does. That is the advantage of an Orthogonal Instruction Set.

Non-Orthogonal Instruction Sets are usually more compact but do not always operate uniformly on their operands. For instance, the Z8018x™ ADD instruction for 8 bit values affects the S & Z bits while the 16 bit ADD does not[1]. The same is true for the INCrement and DECrement instructions. Other processors have similar operations. So, unless you do a lot of assembly language programming for these processors (and you have a good memory!), you will need a complete instruction set reference to know which instructions affect the condition codes and which do not.

It is important to keep in mind that the definitions and rules below are for this processor. Other processors will have similar definitions and rules.

Another few definitions:

Argument	A part of an instruction defining a value to use. A synonym might be parameter.
Operand	The actual value on which the instruction will operate.
Source	The first argument in a two argument instruction. This value does not get modified.

1 Z8018x Family MPU User Manual UM005003-0703

Destination	The second argument in a two argument instruction or the only argument in most single argument instruction. This value will usually get modified.
Read-modify-write	A set of operations performed on a memory location where it is first read, then modified and then written back. The destination operand is often handled this way.

Here is a review of some of the characteristics of the registers.

- Processor characteristics
  - 16 sets of 4 registers each
  - Each register is eight bytes (64 bits)
  - Only the bytes specified (starting with byte 0) by the size value in the instruction will be affected.
- Assembler characteristics
  - Register set names: rs0..rs15 and RS0..RS15
  - Register names: r0..r3 and R0..R3
  - The source operand is the first operand of a two operand instruction
  - The names of the instructions are not case sensitive
  - The operand size, in bytes, is specified by following the instruction name with a period and a single digit
    - .1 = 1 byte
    - .2 = 2 bytes
    - .4 = 4 bytes – this is the value to use when referencing an address
    - .8 = 8 bytes

Keep in mind that this is a Little Endian processor: byte 0 of a multi-byte value is located at the lowest address. This is important to remember when copying values to and from memory.

Condition Codes

In general, the condition codes are affected by all arithmetic and logical instructions. The notation used in describing how the instruction affects the codes is as follows:

0 = value is cleared
1 = value is set
n = value is not changed
x = value is set or cleared based on the result of the operation

Address Mode Timing

The timing of any instruction can be summarized as follows:

instruction fetch + argument(s) + operation

Most processors will use the same basic formula for calculating the number of clocks for its instructions. However, details can be quite different. For instance, some processors use 2 (or more) clock cycles for each memory access. Some may use pipelining to reduce the number of clocks by overlapping instructions. Some may require an extra clock for writing.

- Instruction fetch is always 1 clock
- The operation is usually 1 clock except for the more complex instructions
- The argument times will vary based on the address mode(s) used
- Reading and writing memory takes extra clocks
  - 1 byte = 1 clock
  - 2 bytes = 1 clock
  - 4 bytes = 2 clocks
  - 8 bytes = 4 clocks
  - the number of clocks to read/write from/to memory will be referred to using **K** in the instruction descriptions

The additional clock cycles required for the address modes are listed here:

R = Read, R/W = Read or Write, RMW = Read-Modify-Write

Register = +0

No further memory cycles are required since the data is in a CPU register.

Register indirect = R/W: + K; RMW: + 2 · K

The register contains the address of the value so additional memory cycles are required to access the operand.

Offset = R/W: + 2 + K; RMW: + 2 + 2 · K

The +2 is due to having to read the 2 byte offset value (+1) and to then add (+1) it to the register content. The result of this calculation is then used as the address to access the operand.

Immediate = R: + K

The operand is read from the memory which immediately follows the instruction.

Absolute = R/W: + 2 + K; RMW: + 2 + 2 · K

The +2 is due to having to read the 4 byte address of the operand.

Detailed examples of timing calculation

For these examples only argument one (the source) is varied while argument two is always register mode.

Total clocks = instruction fetch + argument one + argument two + operation

```
add.x   r0, r1          ; argument one = register mode
                        ; total clocks = 1+0+0+1
add.x   (r0), r1        ; argument one = register indirect
                        ; mode
                        ; total clocks = 1+K+0+1
add.x   offset(r0), r1  ; argument one = register offset
                        ; mode
                        ; total clocks = 1+(2+K)+0+1
add.x   #value, r1      ; argument one = immediate mode
                        ; total clocks = 1+K+0+1
add.x   Value, r1       ; argument one = address absolute
                        ; mode
                        ; total clocks = 1+(2+K)+0+1
```

Varying the argument two (the destination) mode: Note that the factor 2·K is required by the destination because the value must be read from memory first to perform the operation and then written back to memory.

```
add.x    r0, (r1)          ; argument two = register indirect
                           ; mode
                           ; total clocks = 1+0+2*K+1
add.x    r0, offset(r1)    ; argument two = register offset
                           ; mode
                           ; total clocks = 1+0+(2+2*K)+1
add.x    r0, Value1        ; argument two = address absolute
                           ; mode
                           ; total clocks = 1+0+(2+2*K)+1
```

Here is an example using offset addressing for both arguments:

```
add.4       offset_1(r0), offset_2(r1)
            ; K = 2,
            ; total clocks = 1+(2+K)+(2+2*K)+1=1+4+6+1=12
```

Detailed Timing Analysis of the instruction, the number of clocks is shown first in each line:

1 – read the instruction
1 – read the argument one offset
1 – add the offset to R0 to create the operand one address
2 – read the 4 byte operand one at the calculated address
1 – read the argument two offset
1 – add the offset to R1 to create the operand two address
2 – read the 4 byte operand two at the calculated address
1 – add the operands
2 – write the 4 byte calculated value to the operand two address

Fig. 8.1

		Argument 2 Mode			
		Register	Register Indirect	Offset	Absolute
Argument 1 Mode	Register	0	2 * K	2 + 2 * K	2 + 2 * K
	Register Indirect	K	3 * K	2 + 3 * K	2 + 3 * K
	Offset	2 + K	2 + 3 * K	4 + 3 * K	4 + 3 * K
	Immediate	K	3 * K	2 + 3 * K	2 + 3 * K
	Absolute	2 + K	2 + 3 * K	4 + 3 * K	4 + 3 * K
data size:		.1 : K=1	.2: K=1	.4: K=2	.8: K=4

The table of Fig. 8.1 (previous page) summarizes all the valid address mode combinations for arguments one and two. To calculate the total instruction time, you still need to add the instruction fetch (always 1 clock) and execution times.
Use the intersection of the argument modes for Double Operand Integer instructions. For most Single Operand instructions use argument two mode with an implied Register Mode for argument one.

Instruction Length

The length of any instruction can be summarized as follows:

instruction + argument(s)

The length of an instruction is always an even number of bytes. The "base" instruction, also called opcode, is always 2 bytes. Additional bytes may be required due to addressing modes and/or operands required by the instruction. As in the case of address mode timing, the additional length due to the address mode is dependent on the mode:

Register = +0

Register indirect = +0

Offset = +2

Immediate (source only) = +<nbr of bytes>

1 byte = +2

2 bytes = +2

4 bytes = +4

8 bytes = +8

Absolute = +4

The length of an instruction will be noted as **B** in the instruction examples

Detailed examples of length calculation

Varying the argument one mode, length in bytes:

```
copy.x  r0, r1           ; argument one = register mode
                         ; B = 2+0+0
```

```
copy.x  (r0), rl          ; argument one = register indirect
                          ; mode
                          ; B = 2+0+0
copy.x  offset(r0), rl    ; argument one = register offset
                          ; mode
                          ; B = 2+2+0
copy.x  #value, rl        ; argument one = immediate mode
                          ; B = 2+L+0
                          ; L is dependent on the operand size
                          ; specified by the ".x"
copy.x  Value, rl         ; argument one = address absolute
                          ; mode
                          ; B = 2+4+0
```

Varying the destination mode:

```
copy.x  r0, (rl)          ; argument two = register indirect
                          ; mode
                          ; B = 2+0+0
copy.x  r0, offset(rl)    ; argument two = register offset
                          ; mode
                          ; B = 2+0+2
copy.x  r0, Valuel        ; argument two = address absolute
                          ; mode
                          ; B = 2+0+4
```

Here is an example using offset addressing for both arguments:

```
copy.4     offset_1(r0), offset_2(rl)    ; B = 2+2+2
```

Instruction Format

The COPY instruction will be described here in detail as an example. The example statement will be followed by a line with the appropriate values of **K** (based on the operand size), the instruction execution time (**T**) in clock cycles and the instruction length (**B**) in bytes. Due to the symmetry between the operand length (**L**) and the number of clock cycles (**K**) it takes to access an operand, in most cases: $L = 2 \cdot K$.

COPY: Copy the value of operand one to the argument two location. The operand one value is not affected.

Execution Time: 1 + argument one + argument two + 0

Condition Codes:

N = x: = value of MSB
Z = x: = 1 if value = 0
C = n
V = n

Example:

```
copy.2      #15, R0          ; copy a 2 byte value of 15 to
                             ; register 0
                             ; K=1, T=1+K+0+0=2, B=2+2*K+0=4
```

Here is another example just to get you thinking a little:

```
copy.1      #15, R0          ; copy a 1 byte value of 15 to
                             ; register 0
                             ; K=1, T=1+K+0+0=2, B=2+2*K+0=4
```

What is the difference between these two instructions? Timing is the same. Length is the same. The only difference is that the first example writes to the lower two bytes of R0 while the second example writes only to the lowest byte of R0. In many cases this is probably not important, but there will be times when it is important.

Most of the example instructions that use immediate mode do not specify the radix – see the **ADD** instruction below. In this case the assumption is that the default radix of 10 is being used. Where the radix is important the operand will specify it – see the **AND** instruction below.

Double Operand Integer

These are the primary arithmetic and logical instructions.

For all of the Double Operand Integer Instructions:

- Operand one (the source) is not affected by the operation.
- Operand two (the destination) receives the result of the instruction (unless otherwise noted) and is handled using a read-modify-write operation.
- The examples will not generally show the state of unused upper bytes in a register. For instance: an instruction specifying a data length of one byte using a register will not show the contents of the upper seven bytes.
- Only the condition which causes the condition codes to be set will be described.

The example for some instructions will be expanded to make them more clear.

Length (in bytes) = 2 + argument one + argument two.

The Operation Clocks value is the additional clocks required to perform the operation.

The Total Execution Time = Instruction Fetch + argument one + argument two + Operation Clocks.

Reminder: **K** = the number of clocks required to read an operand from memory.

Important: there are only two instructions that allow the Stack Pointer (SP) to be used: ADD and COPY. In order to simplify coding the instructions the decision was made to cause the SP to be signified by a value of 3, thus replacing R3. What this means is that these instructions do not allow the SP to be used in the same instruction with register 3 as the other argument. Any instruction that references a register will have that register number as part of the opcode.

ADD: Add the operands using twos-complement arithmetic.

This instruction allows the Stack Pointer (SP) to be either or both arguments with the restriction that register 3 cannot be used for the other argument.

Operation Clocks: 1

Example:

```
add.2      #15, R0        ; add the 2 byte value 15 and the
                          ; contents of R0.
                          ; K=1, T=1+K+0+1=3, B=2+2*K+0=4
```

Condition Codes:

N = x: = value of the result MSB: = 1 if result is negative
Z = x: = 1 if result = 0
C = x: Only valid for *unsigned* values:
C = 1 if the result does not fit in the specified data size

V = x: Only valid for signed operands:
V = 1 if both operands are the same sign but the result is the opposite sign

Note that is is possible for both the C-bit and the V-bit to be set by the same instruction.

AND: Perform the logical-and operation using the 2 operands.

Operation Clocks: 1

Example:

```
and.1       #0x95, R0       ; "and" the 1 byte value 0x95
                            ; (hexadecimal) with the contents
                            ; of R0, store the result in R0
                            ; K=1, T=1+K+0+1=3, B=2+2*K+0=4
```

Fig. 8.2

R0 Before	0xC3	0b11000011	
	0x95	0b10010101	
R0 After	0x81	0b10000001	N=1, Z=0

Another way of thinking of the AND operation is: for each "1" bit in the source – do not change that bit of the destination, for each "0" bit in the source – clear that bit of the destination.

Condition Codes:

N = x: = value of the result MSB: = 1 if result is negative
Z = x: = 1 if result = 0
C = n
V = n

ASHIFT: Shift operand two by the number of bits specified by operand one.

- Positive Shift
  - Essentially a multiplication by a power of two – as long as it fits in the specified data size
  - Shifts left
  - 0 is shifted into the LSB(s)
  - Sign bit is not changed
  - The MSB-1 is lost with each shift
- Negative Shift

Essentially division by a power of two – until the result becomes -1 or 0

Shifts right

The LSB(s) shifts out and is(are) lost

Sign bit is replicated into the next lower bit(s)

Operation Clocks: 2

Example:

```
ashift.2   #5, R0          ; shift the 2 byte value in R0 by 5
                           ; bits to the left
                           ; K=1, T=1+K+0+2=4, B=2+2*K+0=4
```

Fig. 8.3

R0 Before	0x00C3	0b0000000011000011	
R0 After	0x1860	0b0001100001100000	N=0, Z=0, C=0

Condition Codes:

N = n
Z = x: = 1 if result = 0
C = x: = 1 if an attempt is made to change the sign bit
V = n

Notes:

It is possible to shift a positive number in either direction until it becomes 0.

It is not possible to shift a negative number until it becomes 0.

The C-bit will get set only on positive shifts and only if the MSB-1 is a 1 before a shift.

BITEST: Test the state of specified bits by performing a logical-and of the two operands. Only the condition codes are affected. This performs the same operation as the AND instruction except that no operands are modified. This instruction will usually followed by either the BCS or BCC conditional branch instructions. BEQ and BNE could be used instead but the logic is inverted.

Operation Clocks: 1

Note on timing: since the destination is not modified, the $2 \cdot K$ factor is replaced by $1 \cdot K$.

Example:

```
bitest.1    #BIT03, PPODATA ; check the state of bit 3 in the
                            ; low byte of PPODATA
                            ; K= 1, T=1+K+(2+K)+1=6,
                            ; B=2+2*K+4=8
```

Condition Codes:

N = x: = 1 only if the MSB in both operands is set
Z = x: = 1 if result = 0
C = x: = 1 if any of the bits are set, = 0 if none of the bits are set.
V = n

Notes:

BIT03 is a macro that is #define'd as 0x0008 in Processor_Definitions.h.

A more efficient instruction that would do the same thing since the the first operand contains only a single set bit and the second argument is an I/O address is the **IOTST** instruction. It is 4 bytes shorter and 2 clock cycles faster.

COMP: Compare operand one with operand two. This is done by essentially subtracting operand one – operand two. Note that the operands are "subtracted" in the opposite order as compared to the subtract instruction. Only the condition codes are affected. This instruction is usually followed by a conditional branch instruction. The type of branch – signed vs. unsigned – will depend on the type of arguments being compared.

The **COMP** instruction allows immediate mode for the 2nd argument.

Operation Clocks: 1

Note on timing: since the destination is not modified, the $2 \cdot K$ factor is replaced by $1 \cdot K$.

Example:

```
comp.2      R0, #15         ; compare the contents of R0 with
                            ; the 2 byte value 15
                            ; K=1, T=1+0+K+1=3, B=2+2*K+0=4
```

Condition Codes:

N = x: = 1 if the result is < 0
Z = x: = 1 if the result is = 0
C = x: Only valid for *unsigned* values:
C = 1 if a borrow was necessary
V = x: Only valid for *signed* values:
V = 1 if the operands have different signs and the sign of the result is the same as argument two

Note that is is possible for both the C-bit and the V-bit to be set by the same instruction.

COPY: Copy the contents of operand one to the argument two location.

This instruction allows the Stack Pointer (SP) to be either or both arguments with the restriction that register 3 cannot be used for the other argument.

Operation Clocks: 0

Note on timing: since the original value of the destination is not needed, the 2 · K factor is replaced by 1 · K.

Example:

```
copy.2      #15, R0          ; copy a 2 byte value of 15
                             ; (decimal) to R0
                             ; K=1, T=1+K+0+1=3, B=2+2*K+0=4
```

Condition Codes:

N = x: = value of the result MSB: = 1 if value is negative
Z = x: = 1 if value = 0
C = n
V = n

DIV: Divide operand one into operand two. If argument two is a register and the data size is one, two or four the remainder is stored in the adjacent <data size> bytes of the register. Otherwise the remainder is lost.

Operation Clocks: 10

Example:

```
div.2       #15, R0          ; divide the 2 byte value 15 into
                             ; the contents of R0, store the
                             ; result in bytes 0 and 1 of R0
```

```
                                ; with ; the remainder in bytes
                                ; 2 & 3
                                ; K=1, T=1+K+0+10=12, B=2+2*K+0=4
```

Condition Codes:

N = x: = value of the result MSB: = 1 if result is negative
Z = x: = 1 if result = 0
C = x: = 1 for an attempt to divide by 0
V = n

DIVU: Divide operand one into operand two as unsigned. If argument two is a register and the data size is one, two or four, the remainder is stored in the adjacent <data size> bytes of the register. Otherwise the remainder is lost.

Operation Clocks: 10

Example:

```
divu.2      #15, R0         ; divide the 2 byte value 15 into
                            ; the contents of R0, store the
                            ; result in R0 with the remainder
                            ; in bytes 2 & 3
                            ; K=1, T=1+K+0+10=12, B=2+2*K+0=4
```

Condition Codes:

N = x: = value of the result MSB
Z = x: = 1 if result = 0
C = x: = 1 for an attempt to divide by 0
V = n

MUL: Multiply the two operands. If the destination is a register, the result is twice the specified data size (except for the case where data size is eight) using the adjacent <data size> bytes of the register.

Operation Clocks: 5

Example:

```
mul.2       #15, R0         ; multiply the 2 byte value in R0
                            ; by 15, store the result in R0 as
                            ; 4 bytes
                            ; K=1, T=1+K+0+5=7, B=2+2*K+0=4
```

Condition Codes:

N = x: = value of the result MSB: = 1 if result is negative
Z = x: = 1 if result = 0
C = x: = 1 if the result does not fit in the specified <data size * 2> bytes
V = n

MULU: Multiply the two operands as unsigned values. If the destination is a register, the result is twice the specified data size (except for the case where data size is eight). In this case the adjacent <data size> bytes of the register will be used.

Operation Clocks: 5

Example:

```
mulu.2      #15, R0            ; multiply the 2 byte value in R0
                               ; by 15 as unsigned values, store
                               ; the result in R0 as 4 bytes
                               ; K=1, T=1+K+0+5=7, B=2+2*K+0=4
```

Condition Codes:

N = x: = value of the result MSB
Z = x: = 1 if result = 0
C = x: = 1 if the result does not fit in the specified <data size * 2> bytes
V = n

OR: Perform the logical or operation on the two operands.

Operation Clocks: 1

Example:

```
or.1        #0x95, R0          ; or the 1 byte value 0x95 with the
                               ; contents of R0, store result in R0
                               ; K=1, T=1+K+0+1=3, B=2+2*K+0=4
```

Fig. 8.4

R0 Before	0xC3	0b11000011	
	0x95	0b10010101	
R0 After	0xD7	0b11010111	N=1, Z=0

Another way of thinking of the OR operation is: for each "1" bit in the source – set that bit in the destination, for each "0" bit in the source – do not change that bit of the destination.

Condition Codes:

N = x: = value of the result MSB: = 1 if result is negative
Z = x: = 1 if result = 0
C = n
V = n

SUB: Subtract operand one from operand two. Note that the operands are subtracted in the opposite order as compared to the **COMP**are instruction.

Operation Clocks: 1

Example:

```
sub.2       #15, R0         ; subtract the 2 byte value 15 from
                            ; the contents of R0, store the
                            ; result in R0
                            ; K=1, T=1+K+0+1=3, B=2+2*K+0=4
```

Condition Codes:

N = x: = value of the result MSB: = 1 if result is negative
Z = x: = 1 if the result is = 0
C = x: Only valid for *unsigned* values:
C = 1 if a borrow was necessary
V = x: Only valid for *signed* values:
V = 1 if the operands have different signs and the sign of the result is the same as argument one

Note that is is possible for both the C-bit and the V-bit to be set by the same instruction.

XOR: Perform the logical exclusive-or operation on the two operands.

Operation Clocks: 1

Example:

```
xor.1       #0x95, R0       ; xor the 1 byte value 0x95 with
                            ; the contents of R0, store the
                            ; result in R0
                            ; K=1, T=1+K+0+1=3, B=2+2*K+0=4
```

Fig. 8.5

R0 Before	0xC3	0b11000011	
	0x95	0b10010101	
R0 After	0x56	0b01010110	N=0, Z=0

Another way of thinking of the XOR operation is: for each "1" bit in the source – invert that bit in the destination, for each "0" bit in the source – do not change that bit of the destination. In high level languages, inverting an integer value is sometimes accomplished by "exclusive-or"ing it with a 0xFFFF.

Condition Codes:

N = x: = value of the result MSB: = 1 if result is negative
Z = x: = 1 if result = 0
C = n
V = n

Single Operand Integer

For the Single Operand Integer Instructions unless otherwise noted:

The operand is handled using a read-modify-write operation

Only the condition which causes the condition codes to be set will be described

Length = 2 + argument

The Operation Clocks value is the additional clocks required to perform the operation

The Total Execution Time = Instruction Fetch + argument + Operation Clocks

Fig. 8.6 Table of Address Mode Timing and Length: Argument Clock Cycles and Bytes Single Operand Integer

	Register	Register Indirect	Offset	Immediate	Address Absolute
Timing	0	2 * K	2 + 2 * K	K	2 + 2 * K
Length	0	0	2	size value	4

Note: Unless otherwise noted, Single Operand Integer instructions do not allow immediate mode.

ADDC: Add the C-bit to the operand. This instruction is only needed when implementing extended precision arithmetic and usually follows **ADD**ing of the previous <size value> lower bytes. For this processor, the main reason for executing this instruction will be if the resultant data values are greater than eight bytes.

Operation Clocks: 1

Example:

```
addc.2      R0              ; add the C-bit to the contents of
                            ; R0
                            ; K=1, T=1+0+1=2, B=2+0=2
```

See the example in Chapter 4, the section on Condition Codes, for an example of adding two 16 bit values using 8 bit registers.

Condition Codes:

N = x: = value of the result MSB: = 1 if result is negative
Z = x: = 1 if result = 0
C = x: Only valid for unsigned values:
C = 1 if the result does not fit in the specified data size
V = x: Only valid for signed values:
V = 1 if both operands are > 0 and the result is < 0
V = 1 if both operands are < 0 and the result is > 0

CLR: Set the operand to 0.

Operation Clocks: 0

Note on timing: since the original value of the operand is not needed, the $2 \cdot K$ factor is replaced by $1 \cdot K$.

Example:

```
clr.2       R0              ; R0 = 0; K=1, T=1+0+0=1, B=2+0=2
```

N = 0
Z = 1
C = 0
V = 0

COM: Replace the operand with its 2's-complement – basically multiply the operand by –1.

Operation Clocks: 1

Example:

```
com.1       R0              ; generate the 2's-complement of
                            ; the lowest 1 byte contents of R0
                            ; K=1, T=1+0+1=2, B=2+0=2
```

Fig. 8.7

R0 Before	0x15	0b00010101	
R0 After	0xEB	0b11101011	N=1, Z=0

Condition Codes:

N = x: = value of the result MSB: = 1 if result is negative
Z = x: = 1 if result = 0 (this will only happen if the original value is 0)
C = n
V = n

DEC: Subtract one from the operand.

Operation Clocks: 1

Example:

```
dec.2       R0              ; subtract one from the lower 2
                            ; byte contents of R0
                            ; K=1, T=1+0+1=2, B=2+0=2
```

Condition Codes:

N = x: = value of the result MSB: = 1 if result is negative
Z = x: = 1 if result = 0
C = n
V = x: = 1 if result is different sign than original value

DECP: Subtract the size value from the operand. For most applications the operand mode will be register. This instruction is most useful when the program is stepping through a table of values and a register is being used as a pointer to the table.

For instance, if you are working your way through a table which has elements that are four bytes each, the pointer will need to be decremented by four following each access. Using this instruction is faster and takes less memory than the equivalent **ADD** instruction.

Operation Clocks: 1

Example:

```
decp.2      R0          ; subtract 2 from the lower 4 byte
                        ; contents of R0
                        ; K=2, T=1+0+1=1, B=2+0=2
```

Condition Codes:

N = x: = value of the result MSB: = 1 if result is negative
Z = x: = 1 if result = 0
C = n: since the value is a pointer, the C bit does not have meaning
V = n: since a pointer is unsigned by definition

INC: Add one to the operand.

Operation Clocks: 1

Example:

```
inc.2       R0          ; add 1 to the lower 2 byte
                        ; contents of R0
                        ; K=1, T=1+0+1=1, B=2+0=2
```

Condition Codes:

N = x: = value of the result MSB: = 1 if result is negative
Z = x: = 1 if result = 0
C = n
V = x: = 1 if result is different sign than original value

INCP: Add the size value to the operand. For most applications the operand mode will be register. This instruction is most useful when the program is stepping through a table of values and a register is being used as a pointer to the table.

See the **DECP** instruction for more information.

Operation Clocks: 1

Example:

```
incp.2      R0          ; add 2 to the lower 4 byte
                        ; contents of R0
                        ; K=2, T=1+0+1=1, B=2+0=2
```

Condition Codes:

N = x: = value of the result MSB: = 1 if result is negative
Z = x: = 1 if result = 0
C = n: since the value is a pointer, the C bit does not have meaning
V = n: since a pointer is unsigned by definition

INV: Replace the operand with its 1's-complement.

Operation Clocks: 1

Example:

```
inv.1       R0              ; invert each bit of the lowest 1
                            ; byte contents of R0
                            ; K=1, T=1+0+1=1, B=2+0=2
```

Fig. 8.8

R0 Before	0xEA	0b11101010	
R0 After	0x15	0b00010101	N=0, Z=0

Condition Codes:

N = x: = value of the result MSB: = 1 if result is negative
Z = x: = 1 if result = 0 (this will happen only when the original value is –1, all bits set)
C = n
V = n

POP: Copy the operand from the stack, the source is (SP). Add the size value to the SP. Only even numbers of bytes can be pushed and popped. Therefore, the size values can be only: two, four, and eight. K = size value/2.

Operation Clocks: 0

Execution Time: 1 + K + argument + 1

Notes on timing: Since the original value of the operand is not needed, the 2 · K factor is replaced by 1 · K. The additional +1 is due to having to update the Stack Pointer.

Length: 2 + argument

Example:

```
pop.2       R0              ; using SP as the address, copy 2
                            ; bytes to the destination. Add 2
```

```
                                ; to the SP
                                ; K=1, T=1+K+0+1=3, B=2+0=2
```

Fig. 8.9

	SP	(SP)	R0
Before	0x12345678	10	????
After	0x1234567A	????	10

This instruction is equivalent to:

```
copy.2      (SP), R0
add.4       #2, SP              ; remember that the SP is a 4 byte value
```

Condition Codes:

N = x: = value of the operand MSB: = 1 if operand is negative
Z = x: = 1 if operand = 0
C = n, V = n

PUSH: Subtract the size value from the SP then copy the operand onto the stack. Only even numbers of bytes can be pushed and popped. Therefore, the size values can be only: two, four, and eight. K = size value/2.

Note: Immediate Mode is allowed for this instruction.

Operation Clocks: 0

Execution Time: 1 + argument + K + 1

Note on timing: Since the original value of the destination is not needed, the $2 \cdot K$ factor is replaced by $1 \cdot K$. The additional +1 is due to having to update the Stack Pointer.

Length: 2 + argument size

Example:

```
push.2      R0                  ; Decrement SP by 2. Copy the lower
                                ; 2 bytes of R0 onto the stack
                                ; K=1, T=1+0+K+1=3, B=1+0=1
```

Fig. 8.10

	SP	(SP)	R0
Before	0x12345678	????	50
After	0x12345676	50	50

This instruction is equivalent to:

```
add.4      #-2, SP          ; remember that the SP is a 4 byte
                            ; value
copy.2     R0, (SP)
```

Condition Codes:

N = x: = value of the operand MSB: = 1 if operand is negative
Z = x: = 1 if operand = 0
C = n
V = n

SUBC: Subtract the C-bit from the operand. This instruction is only needed when implementing extended precision arithmetic and usually follows **SUB**tracting of the previous <size value> lower bytes. For this processor, the main reason for executing this instruction will be if the data values are greater than eight bytes. See the **ADDC** instruction for more information.

Operation Clocks: 1

Example:

```
subc.2     R0               ; subtract the C-bit from the
                            ; contents of R0
                            ; K=1, T=1+0+1=2, B=2+0=2
```

Condition Codes:

N = x: = value of the result MSB: = 1 if result is negative
Z = x: = 1 if result = 0
C = x: Only valid for unsigned values:
C = 1 if the result does not fit in the specified data size

V = x: Only valid for signed values:
V = 1 if both values are > 0 and the result is < 0
V = 1 if both values are < 0 and the result is > 0

SWAP: Swap the order of the bytes.

Operation Clocks: 1

The size value is used to determine which bytes to swap:

Size = 1: 0<->1
Size = 2: 0,1<->2,3
Size = 4: 0...3<->4...7
Size = 8: not allowed

Examples:

```
swap.1      R1           ; swap 1 byte: byte 0 with byte 1
swap.2      R2           ; swap 2 bytes: bytes 1,0 with
                         ; bytes 3,2
swap.4      R3           ; swap 4 bytes: bytes 3,2,1,0 with
                         ; bytes 7,6,5,4
                         ; K = don't care, T=1+0+1=2, B=2
```

This table shows these instructions using values:

Fig. 8.11

	R1	R2	R3
Before	0x33221100	0x33221100	0x7766554433221100
After	0x33220011	0x11003322	0x3322110077665544

Note that it takes 2 hexadecimal digits to represent 1 byte.

Condition Codes:

N = x: = value of the result MSB: = 1 if result is negative
based on the lowest <data size> value after the swap
Z = x: = 1 if result = 0
based on the lowest <data size> value after the swap
C = n
V = n

SXT: Extend the sign bit. Create the next size larger operand by replicating the sign bit of the operand into all the prepended bits.

The following table details each valid option:

sxt.1: bit 7 is replicated into the next byte: bits 8 – 15
sxt.2: bit 15 is replicated into the next 2 bytes: bits 16 – 31
sxt.4: bit 31 is replicated into the next 4 bytes: bits 32 – 63

The effect of this instruction is similar to the C feature of casting an integer to the next larger size. Note that sxt.8 is not valid since this processor does not support 128 bit integers.

Operation Clocks: 1

Example:

```
sxt.1       R0               ; replicate bit 7 into bits 8 - 15
                             ; K=1, T=1+1=2, B=2+0=2
```

Fig. 8.12

R0 Before	0x??EA
R0 After	0xFFEA

Condition Codes:

N = x: = value of the result MSB: = 1 if result is negative
Z = x: = 1 if result = 0
C = 0
V = 0

TEST: Test the operand for zero and sign.

Operation Clocks: 0

Note on timing: since the value of the destination is not modified, the 2 ·K factor is replaced by 1 · K.

Example:

```
test.2      R0               ; test R0 for 0 and sign
                             ; K=1, T=1+0=1, B=2+0=2
```

Condition Codes:

N = x: = value of the result MSB: = 1 if result is negative
Z = x: = 1 if result = 0
C = 0
V = 0

Rotate

The Rotate instructions are a subset of the Single Operand Integer instructions. For all of the Rotate Instructions, the operand is handled using a read-modify-write operation. With a rotate instruction, the unit being rotated has the MSB essentially right next to bit 0. A rotate using the C-bit would place the C-bit between the MSB and bit 0. One way to view this is to think of the unit as a circle as in the diagram. No bits are lost with a rotate.

The diagram depicts a rotate left without the C-bit. A rotate right would look identical except with the arrow pointing to bit 1.

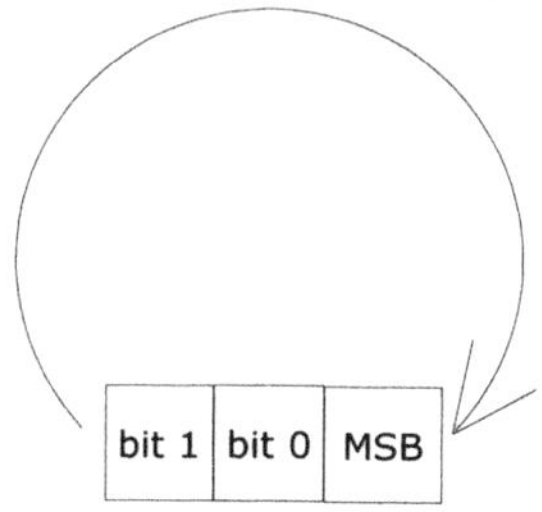

Fig. 8.13

RL: Rotate the operand one bit to the left. The MSB is rotated into bit 0.

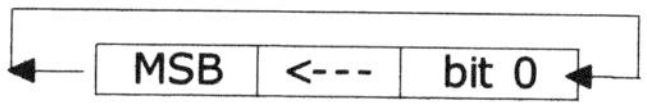

Fig. 8.14

Operation Clocks: 1

Example:

```
rl.2        R0              ; rotate the lower 2 bytes of r0 by
                            ; 1 bit to the left
                            ; K=1, T=1+0=1, B=2+0=2
```

Condition Codes:

N = x: = value of the result MSB: = 1 if result is negative
Z = x: = 1 if result = 0
C = n
V = n

RLC: Rotate the operand one bit to the left thru the C-bit. The MSB is rotated into the C-bit. The C-bit is rotated into bit 0.

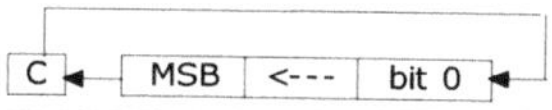

Fig. 8.15

Operation Clocks: 1

Example:

```
rl.2        R0                ; rotate the lower 2 bytes of r0
                              ; through the C-bit by 1 bit to the left
                              ; K=1, T=1+0=1, B=2+0=2
```

Condition Codes:

N = x: = value of the result MSB: = 1 if result is negative
Z = x: = 1 if result = 0
C = x: = value of original MSB
V = n

RR: Rotate the operand one bit to the right. Bit 0 is rotated into the MSB.

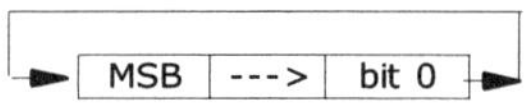

Fig. 8.16

Operation Clocks: 1

Example:

```
rr.2        R0                ; rotate the lower 2 bytes of r0
                              ; through the C-bit by 1 bit to the
                              ; right
                              ; K=1, T=1+0=1, B=2+0=2
```

Condition Codes:

N = x: = value of the result MSB: = 1 if result is negative
Z = x: = 1 if result = 0
C = n
V = n

RRC: Rotate the operand one bit to the right thru the C-bit. Bit 0 is rotated into the C-bit. The C-bit is rotated into the MSB.

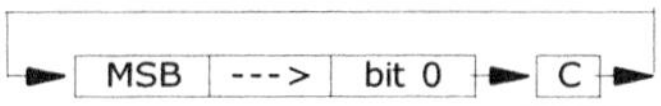

Fig. 8.17

Operation Clocks: 1

Example:

```
rrc.2       R0              ; rotate the lower 2 bytes of r0
                            ; through the C-bit by 1 bit to the
                            ; right
                            ; K=1, T=1+0=1, B=2+0=2
```

Condition Codes:

N = x:	= value of the result MSB: = 1 if result is negative
Z = x:	= 1 if result = 0
C = x:	= value of original bit 0
V = n	

RLB: Rotate the operand one byte to the left.

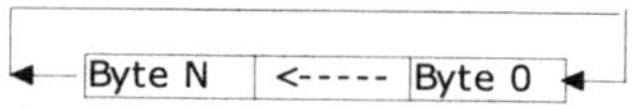

Fig. 8.18

Operation Clocks: 1

Example:

```
rlb.4       R0              ; rotate the lower 4 bytes of r0 by
                            ; 1 byte to the left, byte 3 moves
                            ; into byte 0
                            ; K=1, T=1+0=1, B=2+0=2
```

This would be equivalent to executing an rl.4 R0 eight times.

Condition Codes:

N = x:	= value of the result MSB: = 1 if result is negative
Z = x:	= 1 if result = 0
C = n	
V = n	

RRB: Rotate the operand one byte to the right.

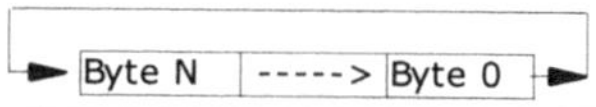

Fig. 8.19

Operation Clocks: 1

Example:

```
rrb.4       R0                ; rotate the lower 4 bytes of r0 by
                              ; 1 byte to the right, byte 0 moves
                              ; into byte 3
                              ; K=1, T=1+0=1, B=2+0=2
```

This would be equivalent to executing an rr.4 R0 eight times.

Condition Codes:

N = x: = value of the result MSB: = 1 if result is negative
Z = x: = 1 if result = 0
C = n
V = n

Shift

The Shift instructions are also a subset of the Single Operand Integer instructions. For all of the Shift Instructions, the operand is handled using a read-modify-write operation.

Arithmetic Shift instructions basically perform a multiply (left shift) or divide (right shift) by two, these instructions do not affect the sign bit. Logical Shifts are similar to rotate instructions except that the MSB is not next to bit 0 – bits get "lost."

SLA: Shift Left Arithmetic. If the MSB-1 is 0, this is a multiply by two. The MSB-1 is lost and bit 0 is loaded with 0.

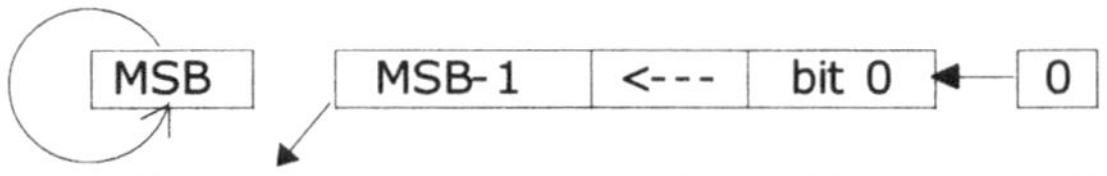

Fig. 8.20

Operation Clocks: 1

Example:

```
sla.2       R0                ; shift the lower 2 bytes of r0 by
                              ; 1 bit to the left
                              ; K=1, T=1+0+1=2, B=2+0=2
```

Condition Codes:

N = x: = value of the result MSB: = 1 if result is negative

Z = x: = 1 if result = 0
C = n
V = n

SLL: Shift Left Logical. The MSB is lost and bit 0 is loaded with 0.

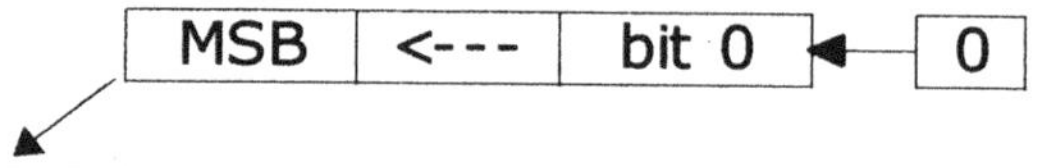

Fig. 8.21

Operation Clocks: 1

Example:

```
sll.2       R0                 ; shift the lower 2 bytes of r0 by
                               ; 1 bit to the left
                               ; K=1, T=1+0+1=2, B=2+0=2
```

Condition Codes:

N = x: = value of the result MSB: = 1 if result is negative
Z = x: = 1 if result = 0
C = n
V = n

SLLC: Shift Left Logical with Carry. The original value of the C-bit is lost, it is loaded with the MSB and bit 0 is loaded with 0.

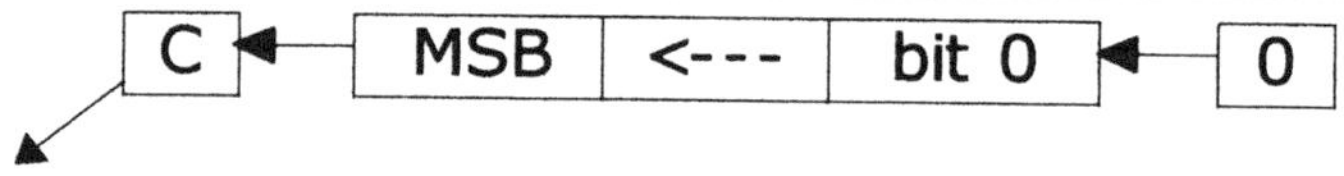

Fig. 8.22

Operation Clocks: 1

Example:

```
sll.2       R0                 ; shift the lower 2 bytes of r0 by
                               ; 1 bit to the left using the C-bit
                               ; K=1, T=1+0+1=2, B=2+0=2
```

Condition Codes:

N = x: = value of the result MSB: = 1 if result is negative
Z = x: = 1 if result = 0
C = x: takes on the original value of the MSB
V = n

SRA: Shift Right Arithmetic . This is a divide by two. The MSB is replicated into itself and the next lower bit. The LSB is lost.

Fig. 8.23

Operation Clocks: 1

Example:

```
sra.2       R0                ; shift the lower 2 bytes of r0 by
                              ; 1 bit to the right
                              ; K=1, T=1+0+1=2, B=2+0=2
```

Condition Codes:

N = x: = value of the result MSB: = 1 if result is negative
Z = x: = 1 if result = 0
C = n
V = n

SRL: Shift Right Logical. The MSB is loaded with 0 and the LSB is lost.

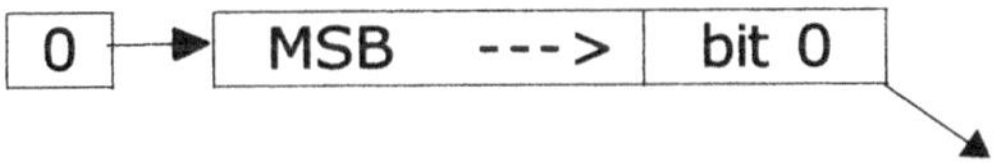

Fig. 8.24

Operation Clocks: 1

Example:

```
srl.2       R0                ; shift the lower 2 bytes of r0 by
                              ; 1 bit to the right
                              ; K=1, T=1+0+1=2, B=2+0=2
```

Condition Codes:

N = x: = 0
Z = x: = 1 if result = 0
C = n
V = n

SRLC: Shift Right Logical with Carry. The MSB is loaded with 0, the LSB shifts into the C-bit, the original value of the C-bit is lost.

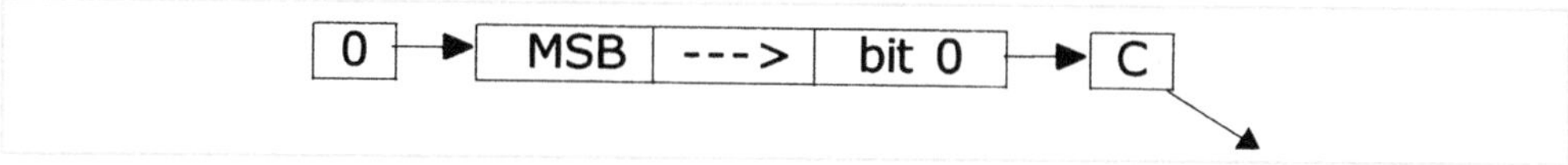

Fig. 8.25

Operation Clocks: 1

Example:

```
srlc.2     R0              ; shift the lower 2 bytes of r0 by
                           ; 1 bit to the right using the C-bit
                           ; K=1, T=1+0+1=2, B=2+0=2
```

Condition Codes:

N = x: = 0
Z = x: = 1 if result = 0
C = x: takes on the original value of the LSB
V = n

Floating Point

Floating Point summary

All floating point values are comprised of 3 parts:

- Sign bit – 0 indicates a positive number.
- Exponent – a power of 2 expressed with a built-in bias value.
- Mantissa – a fraction with each bit representing successively larger negative powers of 2.

There are several web sites (*http://en.wikipedia.org/wiki/IEEE 754-2008* and *http://babbage.cs.qc.edu/IEEE-754/Decimal.html* are just two of many) which describe these formats in great detail but here is a summary:

Fig. 8.26

Sign of the value	Exponent	Mantissa
1 bit	9 (bias = 127) or 11 bits (bias = 1023)	23 or 52 bits

As you can see, floating point values are in sign-magnitude format. Also notice that the exponent has seven bits in the MSByte and one bit in the next lower byte. You can have both a positive and negative representation for 0. There is an industry standard (IEEE 754) which defines all the valid floating point formats. Here are a few more facts about floating point notation:

- Single Precision is 32 bits (or two words or 4 bytes)

- Double Precision is 64 bits (or four words or 8 bytes)

- The actual exponent value is calculated as follows: "real" exponent = exponent – bias value. For instance, if the stored exponent of a single precision value is 122 the "real" exponent is –5 and is calculated as follows:

  $$122 - \text{bias} = 122 - 127 = -5.$$

- The mantissa has a "hidden" bit which represents the value 1. The mantissa always represents a value of:

  $$1.0 \leq X < 2.0$$

- The most significant bit of the mantissa represents the value 2^{-1} (= 1/2), the next lower bit is 2^{-2} (= 1/4), etc.

- Not all values can be represented exactly in floating point since there are a finite number of bits

- You should never test for equality between 2 floating point numbers

- A single precision value has only 6 or 7 decimal digits of accuracy depending on its absolute value

- The largest single precision value is approximately: 3.4028E+38

- The smallest single precision value is approximately: 1.1754E–38

- The largest double precision value is approximately: 1.7976E+308

- The smallest double precision value is approximately: 2.2250E–308

- There are modifications of the standard which trade off bits between the exponent and mantissa to allow either a greater range or more precision using the same number of bits.

The value can be calculated as follows:

$$\text{value} = (-1)^{\text{sign}} \cdot 2^{\text{exponent}-\text{bias}} \cdot (\text{mantissa} + 1.0)$$

Here is an example of single precision floating point showing the representation of the decimal number 1.0:

0x3F800000 →
Sign bit = 0; Exponent = 0x7F = 127; Mantissa = 0 +1.0 (hidden bit)

Using the formula above: $(-1)^0 \cdot 2^{127-\text{bias}} \cdot (0+1.0) = 1 \cdot 2^0 \cdot 1.0 = 1.0$

Floating Point in This Processor

These instructions allow you to operate on both single and double precision floating point values. All floating point instructions have a single argument with an implied second argument of R0. The result of the instructions is stored in R0 unless specifically documented otherwise. The instruction execution time is calculated as follows:

Instruction read (=1) + argument (see table) + Operation clocks (varies by operation).

The instruction length (in bytes) is calculated as follows:

Instruction (=2) + argument (see table).

Notes:

- SP is the abbreviation for Single Precision
- DP is the abbreviation for Double Precision
- The C-bit is not affected by any of the floating point instructions.
- The V-bit is set if the result is Not a Number – a standard error in IEEE 754
- The instructions starting with FPS... are SP
- The instructions starting with FPD... are DP
- K = 2 for SP
- K = 4 for DP

Fig. 8.27 Table of Address Mode Timing and Length: Argument Clock Cycles and Bytes Floating Point

	Register	Register Indirect	Offset	Immediate
Timing	0	K	2 + K	K
Length	0	0	2	size value

Single Precision Floating Point

FPIS: Convert the integer operand to SP and store in R0.

Notes: for this instruction K is dependent on the size of the integer value. Only the integer to floating point instructions allow the argument size specification.

Operation Clocks: 1

Example:

```
fpis.2      #15              ; convert 15 to SP
                             ; K=1 T=1+K+1=3, B=2+2*K=4
```

Condition Codes:

N = x:	= value of the result MSB: = 1 if result is negative
Z = x:	= 1 if result = 0

FPSADD: Add the operand to R0

Operation Clocks: 1

Example:

```
fpsadd      #0f1.5           ; add 1.5 to R0
                             ; T=1+K+1=4, B=2+2*K=4
```

Condition Codes:

N = x:	= value of the result MSB: = 1 if result is negative
Z = x:	= 1 if result = 0

FPSCOMP: Compare the operand with R0 by essentially executing (operand – R0), R0 is not modified. Note that the operands are "subtracted" in the opposite order as compared to the subtract instruction.

Operation Clocks: 1

Example:

```
fpscomp     #0f1.5           ; compare 1.5 with R0
                             ; T=1+K+1=4, B=2+2*K=4
```

Condition Codes:

N = x:	= 1 if operand < R0
Z = x:	= 1 if operand = R0

FPSDIV: Divide R0 by the operand

Operation Clocks: 10

Example:

```
fpsdiv    #0f1.5         ; divide 1.5 into R0
                         ; T=1+K+10=13, B=2+2*K=4
```

Condition Codes:

N = x:	= value of the result MSB: = 1 if result is negative
Z = x:	= 1 if result = 0

FPSDP: Convert the operand to DP

Operation Clocks: 2

Example:

```
fpsdp     R0             ; convert the SP value in R0 to DP
                         ; T=1+0+2=3, B=2+0=2
```

Condition Codes:

N = x:	= value of the result MSB: = 1 if result is negative
Z = x:	= 1 if result = 0

FPSMUL: Multiply R0 by the operand

Operation Clocks: 5

Example:

```
fpsmul    #0f1.5         ; multiply R0 by 1.5
                         ; T=1+K+5=8 ,B=2+2*K=4
```

Condition Codes:

N = x: = value of the result MSB: = 1 if result is negative
Z = x: = 1 if result = 0

FPSI: Convert the SP operand to integer, store the result as a 64 bit integer. This processor uses the typical rules for rounding:

If the fraction is > .5 then round up
If the fraction is < .5 then round down
If the fraction = .5 then make the integer even

Operation Clocks: 1

Example:

```
fpsi        #0f1.5          ; convert the SP number 1.5 to
                            ; integer
                            ; T=1+K+1=4, B=2+2*K=4
```

Condition Codes:

N = x: = value of the result MSB: = 1 if result is negative
Z = x: = 1 if result = 0

FPSSUB: Subtract the operand from R0 (R0 - operand). Note that the operands are "subtracted" in the opposite order as compared to the compare instruction.

Operation Clocks: 1

Example:

```
fpssub      #0f1.5          ; subtract 1.5 from R0
                            ; T=1+K+1=4, B=2+2*K=4
```

Condition Codes:

N = x: = value of the result MSB: = 1 if R0 < operand
Z = x: = 1 if R0 = operand

Double Precision Floating Point

Note: remember that K=4 for DP.

FPID: Convert the integer operand to DP.

Notes: for this instruction K is dependent on the size of the integer value. Only the integer to floating point instructions require the argument size specification.

Operation Clocks: 2

Example:

```
fpid.2      #0f15          ; convert 15 to DP, store the
                           ; result in R0
                           ; K=1, T=1+K+1=3, B=2+2*K=4
```

Condition Codes:

N = x:	= value of the result MSB: = 1 if result is negative
Z = x:	= 1 if result = 0

FPDADD: Add the operand to R0

Operation Clocks: 1

Example:

```
fpdadd      #0f1.5         ; add 1.5 to R0
                           ; T=1+K+1=6, B=2+2*K=10
```

Condition Codes:

N = x:	= value of the result MSB: = 1 if result is negative
Z = x:	= 1 if result = 0

FPDCOMP: Compare the operand with R0 by essentially executing (operand – R0), R0 is not modified. Note that the operands are "subtracted" in the opposite order as compared to the subtract instruction.

Operation Clocks: 1

Example:

```
fpdcomp     #0f1.5         ; compare 1.5 with R0
                           ; T=1+K+1=6, B=2+2*K=10
```

Condition Codes:

N = x:	= 1 if operand < R0
Z = x:	= 1 if operand = R0

FPDI: Convert the DP operand to integer, store the result as a 64 bit value.

Operation Clocks: 1

Example:

```
fpdi        #0f1.5            ; convert the DP number 1.5 to
                              ; integer
                              ; T=1+K+1=6, B=2+2*K=1
```

Condition Codes:

N = x:	= value of the result MSB: = 1 if result is negative
Z = x:	= 1 if result = 0

FPDDIV: Divide R0 by the operand

Operation Clocks: 10

Example:

```
fpddiv      #0f1.5            ; divide R0 by 1.5
                              ; T=1+K+10=15, B=2+2*K=10
```

Condition Codes:

N = x:	= value of the result MSB: = 1 if result is negative
Z = x:	= 1 if result = 0

FPDMUL: Multiply R0 by the operand

Operation Clocks: 5

Example:

```
fpdmul      #0f1.5            ; multiply R0 by 1.5
                              ; T=1+K+5=10, B=2+2*K=10
```

Condition Codes:

N = x:	= value of the result MSB: = 1 if result is negative
Z = x:	= 1 if result = 0

FPDSP: Convert the operand to SP

Operation Clocks: 2

Example:

```
fpdsp      R0              ; convert R0 to SP
                           ; T=1+0+2=3, B=2+0=2
```

Condition Codes:

N = x:	= value of the result MSB: = 1 if result is negative
Z = x:	= 1 if result = 0

FPDSUB: Subtract the operand from R0 (R0 – operand). Note that the operands are "subtracted" in the opposite order as compared to the compare instruction.

Operation Clocks: 1

Example:

```
fpdsub     #0f1.5          ; subtract 1.5 from R0, store the
                           ; result in R0
                           ; T=1+K+1=6, B=2+2*K=10
```

Condition Codes:

N = x:	= 1 if R0 < operand
Z = x:	= 1 if R0 = operand

Register Set

This set of instructions allows the programmer to swap/exchange data in the register sets. Note that

- All of the operands are implied immediate mode
- The entire registers are affected (except **PUSHR** and **POPR**)
- That the syntax requires the register set number without a prefix of "rs"
- Only the **PUSHR** and **POPR** instructions affect the condition codes and allow specification of the data size.

If the programmer decides to use another register set, it is up to the programmer to ensure that there are no conflicts.

Conflicts can occur if another register set is selected in an ISR. Any registers which are used must be saved on the stack and then restored – unlike the registers associated with the IPL. Of course it is also possible that a "rule" can be made for a program that allows an ISR to make use of one or more specific register sets and not have to save them.

RSCOPY: Copy the default register set to the specified register set.

Example:

```
rscopy      2              ; copy the default register set to
                           ; RS2
                           ; T=2, B=2
```

RSDEF: Set the default register set.

Example:

```
rsdef       2              ; set the processor to use RS2 as
                           ; the default
                           ; T=1, B=2
```

RSEXCH: Exchange the default register set with the specified register set.

Example:

```
rsexch      12             ; exchange the default register set
                           ; with RS12
                           ; T=2, B=2
```

RCOPY: Copy a single register to the same one in the specified RS

Example:

```
rcopy   R1, 8       ; copy R1 in the current RS to R1
                ; in RS8
                ; T=1, B=2
```

REXCH: Exchange a single register with the same one in the specified RS.

Example:

```
rexch      R1, 8              ; exchange R1 in the current RS
                              ; with R1 in RS8
                              ; T=1, B=2
```

POPR: Pop the registers specified in the mask (highest register first, bit 0 = R0, bit 1 = R1, etc), from the stack, the source is (SP). Add the size value to the SP for each register popped.

Only even numbers of bytes can be pushed and popped. Therefore, the size values can be only two, four, and eight. K = size value/2.

> *IMPORTANT: if a size of one is specified it will be changed to two.*

Execution Time: $1 + (n \cdot K) + n$ (n = number of registers)

> *Notes on timing: the $(n \cdot K)$ factor is due to having to read K words from memory for each register. The n factor is due to having to update the SP for each register.*

Example:

```
pop.4      0b0011             ; pop R0 and R1 from the stack as 4
                              ; byte values
                              ; K=2, T=1+(2*K)+2=7, B=2
```

This instruction is equivalent to:

```
copy.4     (SP), R1
add.4      #4, SP
copy.4     (SP), R0
add.4      #4, SP
```

Condition Codes:

N = x: the value of the MSB of the last register POP'ed
Z = x: = 1 if the value of the last register POP'ed is 0
C = n
V = n

PUSHR: Push the registers specified in the mask (lowest register first) onto the stack, the destination is (SP). The size value is used to update the SP which will be decremented by the size for each register pushed. Only even numbers of bytes can be pushed and popped. Therefore, the size values can be only two, four and eight. K = size value/2.

> *IMPORTANT: if a size of one is specified it will be changed to two.*

Execution Time: 1 + (n·K) + n (n = number of registers)

Notes on timing: the (n · K) factor is due to having to write K words to memory for each register. The n factor is due to having to update the SP for each register.

Example:

```
push.4     0b0101          ; push R0 and R2 onto the stack as
                           ; 4 byte values
                           ; K=2, T=1+(3*K)+2=9, B=2
```

This instruction is equivalent to:

```
add.4      #-4, SP
copy.4     R0, (SP)
add.4      #-4, SP
copy.4     R2, (SP)
```

Condition Codes:

N = x: the value of the MSB of the last register PUSH'ed
Z = x: = 1 if the value of the last register PUSH'ed is 0
C = n
V = n

Program Counter

The following instructions modify the Program Counter in some way. The instructions do not affect the condition codes.

Jump

Execute an unconditional jump to another address. Both the JMP and CALL instructions allow a register to contain the destination address. In these cases the syntax does not use parentheses surrounding the register designation.

JMP: Jump to a 32 bit absolute address. The destination address can be in a register or explicitly specified.

Examples:

```
jmp     R0              ; jump to the 32 bit address in R0
                        ; T=2 (1 to read the instruction +1
                        ; to modify the PC),B=2
```

```
jmp     Function_1        ; jump to the 32 bit address of
                          ; Function_1
                          ; T=4 (3 to read the instruction +1
                          ; to modify the PC), B=6
```

JMPR: Jump relative to the updated value of the PC. The offset can be in a register or the destination address can be explicitly specified. Rules for when the destination is specified:

- The assembler will calculate the offset value
- The offset value in the instruction (20 bits) is shifted left 1 bit, making a 21 bit signed offset, before adding it to the PC
- The destination must be within approximately 1MB of the current location
- If the destination is too far, an error will be generated

If register mode is being used there is no limit to the offset. This instruction can be used in generating Position Independent Code.

Examples:

```
jmpr    Function_1        ; T=3 (2 to read the instruction +1
                          ; to modify the PC), B=4
        ; offset = ( address of destination - (address of
        ; jmpr instruction + 4) ) / 2
jmpr    R1                ; T=2 (1 to read the instruction +1
                          ; to modify the PC),B=2
        ; offset = address of destination - address of jmpr
        ; instruction + 2
```

JMPS: Jump using a short 21 bit absolute address. Since all instructions must begin on even byte addresses, the address in the instruction (20 bits) is shifted left 1 bit before copying it to the PC. The upper 11 bits of the PC are set to 0.

The destination must be within the lowest 2MB of the memory. If the destination is not within the first 2MB, an error will be generated.

Example:

```
jmps       Function_1       ; T=3 (2 to read the instruction +1
                            ; to modify the PC), B=4
```

Call

Call a function/subroutine by pushing the updated PC onto the stack and then jumping to the specified address. The function must execute an **rets** instruction in order to return to the instruction following the **call**. If a return is not properly executed, the stack will become corrupted and probably cause the program to crash.

Every call instruction incurs a timing increment of 3 clocks in order to push the return address onto the stack: 1 clock to decrement the SP by four, 2 clocks to copy the updated PC to (SP).

If timing is critical to the application, you should account for the **call** as well as the corresponding **rets** instruction.

CALL: Call the function at an absolute 32 bit address. The address can be in a register or the destination address can be explicitly specified.

Examples:

```
call    R0              ; call the function specified by the
                        ; 32 bit address in R0
                        ; T=5 (1 to read the instruction + 3
                        ; to push the PC + 1 to modify the
                        ; PC), B=2
call    Function_1      ; call to the 32 bit address of
                        ; Function_1
                        ; T=7 (3 to read the instruction + 3
                        ; to push the PC + 1 to modify the
                        ; PC), B=6
```

CALLR: Execute a call relative to the current value of the PC. The offset can be in a register or the destination address can be explicitly specified. Rules for when the destination is specified:

- The assembler will calculate the offset value
- The offset value in the instruction (20 bits) is shifted left 1 bit, making a 21 bit signed offset, before adding it to the PC
- The destination must be within approximately 1MB of the current location
- If the destination is too far, an error will be generated

If register mode is being used there is no limit to the offset.

These instructions can be used in generating Position Independent Code.

Examples:

```
callr   Function_1        ; T=6 (2 to read the instruction +
                          ; 3 to push the PC + 1 to modify the
                          ; PC), B=4
        ; offset = ( address of destination - (address of
        ; callr instruction + 4) ) / 2
callr   R0                ; T=5 (1 to read the instruction +
                          ; 3 to push the PC + 1 to modify the
                          ; PC), B=2
        ; offset = address of destination - address of
        ; callr instruction + 2
```

CALLS: Execute a call to a short 21 bit absolute address. Since all instructions must begin on even byte addresses, the address in the instruction (20 bits) is shifted left 1 bit before copying it to the PC. The destination must be within the lowest 2 MB of the memory. If the destination is not within the first 2 MB, an error will be generated.

Example:

```
calls      Function_1        ; T=6 (2 to read the instruction +
                             ; 3 to push the PC + 1 to modify
                             ; the PC) B=4
```

RETS: Return from a subroutine/function. The return address is popped from the stack.

Example:

```
rets                         ; T=5 (1 to read the instruction +
                             ; 3 to pop the return address + 1
                             ; to modify the PC), B=2
```

RETI: Return from an interrupt. The PSR and return address will be popped from the stack, in that order.

When calculating the time it takes to execute an ISR, you should also include the time it takes to acknowledge the interrupt.

Example:

```
reti                         ; T=6 (1 to read the instruction +
                             ; 5 to pop the return address and
                             ; PSR), B=2
```

Here is a detailed analysis of an RTI instruction. The value at the start of each line is the number of clocks required:

- 1 – instruction fetch
- 2 – pop the PSR from the stack
  - 1 – retrieve the PSR from the stack
  - 1 – increment the SP by two
- 3 – pop the PC from the stack
  - 2 – retrieve the PC from the stack
  - 1 – increment the SP by four

Branch

All of the branch instructions are 2 bytes long and are always relative to the address of the instruction following the branch. This is because the Program Counter is incremented during the evaluation of the branch instruction. When the decision to either branch or not branch is made, the PC is already pointing to the next instruction.

The branch instructions all take either 2 or 3 clocks depending on whether or not the branch is taken: 2 if no, 3 if yes. The branch location must be within the range:

$$-256 \text{ bytes} \leq (\text{Branch instruction address} + 2) \leq +254 \text{ bytes}$$

The following two instructions are *usually* used for implementing local loops with the "branch to" location occurring previous to the **DB_E** instruction.

DBGE: Decrement the *signed* word value (2 bytes) in the register and branch if the result is positive.

Example:

```
dbge        R0, Loc_1        ; decrement R0,
                             ; if the result is >= 0 branch to
                             ; Loc_1, else continue to the next
                             ; instruction
```

Condition Codes:

N = x: = value of the result MSB: = 1 if result is negative (branch not taken)
Z = x: = 1 if result = 0
C = n
V = n

Here is a brief "corner value" analysis"

Rx = 1: execute the branch once
–32767 ≤ Rx ≤ 0: branch is not executed
Rx = –32768: branch will be executed 32768 times. This is because when a word value of -32768 is decremented, the result is +32767

DBNE: Decrement the *unsigned* word value (2 bytes) in the register and branch if the result is not equal to 0.

Example:

```
dbne        R0, Loc_1         ; decrement R0, if the result is
                              ; != 0 branch to Loc_1, else
                              ; continue to the next instruction
```

Condition Codes:

N = x: = value of the result MSB: = 1 if result is negative
Z = x: = 1 if result = 0
C = n
V = n

The following set of branch instructions are used to make decisions based usually on the instruction just executed. Some notes about the instructions:

- The condition codes are not affected by these instructions.
- The conditional branches are usually executed after an arithmetic or logical operation.
- The examples will be shown with another instruction which demonstrates usage.
- Most branch instructions operate on signed values, those which operate on unsigned values are noted as such.
- Those branch instructions which are listed as equivalent are not implemented in the assembler.

BR: Unconditional branch

Example:

```
br          Loc_l               ; branch to Loc_l
```

BCC: Branch if "Carry Clear" (C-bit = 0)

Example:

```
rlc.2       R0                  ; rotate r0 1 bit to the left using
                                ; the C-bit
bcc         Loc_l               ; branch to Loc_l if bit 15 of
                                ; original R0 = 0
```

BCS: Branch if "Carry Set" (C-bit = 1)

Example:

```
rlc.2       R0                  ; rotate r0 1 bit to the left using
                                ; the C-bit
bcs         Loc_l               ; branch to Loc_l if bit 15 of
                                ; original R0 = 1
```

BEQ: Branch if equal (Z-bit = 1). An equivalent instruction is **BZS**: branch if "Z-bit is Set".

Example:

```
comp        R0, R1
beq         Loc_l               ; branch to Loc_l if R0 = R1 (Z-bit
                                ; = 1)
```

BGE: Branch if "Greater than or Equal" (C-bit = V-bit). Should be used when comparing *signed* integers.

Example:

```
comp        R0, R1
bge         Loc_l               ; branch to Loc_l if R0 >= R1
```

BGT: Branch if "Greater Than" (Z-bit = 0 && N-bit = V-bit). Should be used when comparing *signed* integers.

Example:

```
comp        R0, R1
bgt         Location_1        ; branch to Loc_1 if R0 > R1
```

BGTU: Branch if "Greater Than, Unsigned" (C-bit = 1 && Z-bit = 0). Should be used when comparing *unsigned* integers.

Example:

```
bgtu        Loc_1             ; branch to Loc_1 if C-bit = 1 &
                              ; Z-bit = 0
```

BLE: Branch if "Less than or Equal" (Z-bit = 1 || N-bit != V-bit). Should be used when comparing *signed* integers.

Example:

```
comp        R0, R1
ble         Loc_1             ; branch to Loc_1 if R0 <= R1
                              ; (Z-bit = 1 or N != V)
```

BLEU: Branch if "Less than or Equal, Unsigned" (C-bit = 0 || Z-bit = 1). Should be used when comparing unsigned integers.

Example:

```
bleu        Loc_1             ; branch to Loc_1 if C-bit = 0 |
                              ; Z-bit = 1
```

BLT: Branch if "Less Than" (N-bit != V-bit). Should be used when comparing *signed* integers.

Example:

```
comp        R0, R1
blt         Loc_1             ; branch to Loc_1 if R0 < R1 (N-bit
                              ; != V-bit)
```

BMI: Branch if minus (N-bit = 1). Should be used when comparing or testing signed integers. An equivalent instruction is BNS: branch if "N-bit is Set".

Example:

```
test        R0
bmi         Loc_1             ; branch to Loc_1 if R0 < 0 (N-bit = 1)
```

BNE: Branch if not equal (Z-bit = 0). An equivalent instruction is BZC: branch if "Z-bit is clear".

Example:

```
comp        R0, R1
bne         Loc_1               ; branch to Loc_1 if R0 != R1
                                ; (Z-bit = 0)
```

BPL: Branch if plus (N-bit = 0). Should be used when comparing or testing signed integers. An equivalent instruction is BNC: branch if "N-bit is Clear".

Example:

```
test        R0
bpl         Loc_1               ; branch to Loc_1 if R0 >= 0
                                ; (N-bit = 0)
```

BVC: Branch if "V-bit is Clear" (V-bit = 0).

Example:

```
bvc         Loc_1               ; branch to Loc_1 if V-bit = 0
```

BVS: Branch if "V-bit is Set" (V-bit = 1).

Example:

```
bvs         Loc_1               ; branch to Loc_1 if V-bit = 1
```

Short I/O

Access the internal I/O devices using shorter and faster instructions. The 16 bit offset into the I/O address area is used instead of the full 32 bit address. The I/O address specified in each of these instructions MUST be Address Absolute mode.

> *IMPORTANT: each of these I/O instructions MUST have an I/O address as an argument. If you want to use either of the register modes for the I/O address reference, you must use the normal single or double operand instructions.*

IOAND: Logically-and the argument with the I/O register. The I/O register is always the second argument – the destination.

This instruction can be used to clear bits in I/O registers.

Execution Time: 1 + argument + 1 + 2 * K + 1

The first +1 is for reading the I/O address, the + 2 ·K is for accessing the I/O device using a read-modify-write cycle, the second +1 is to perform the "and" operation.

Length: 2 + argument one + 2

The +2 is for the I/O address

Example:

```
ioand.1    R0, SP0DATA      ; logically-and 1 byte of R0 with
                            ; Serial Port 0 Data Register
                            ; K=1, T=1+0+1+(2*1)+1=5, B=2+0+2=4
```

Timing Details:

1 = read the instruction
0 = access R0
1 = read the I/O address
1 = read 1 byte from the I/O register
1 = perform the "and" operation
1 = write 1 byte to the I/O device

Condition Codes:

N = x: = value of the result MSB: = 1 if result is negative
Z = x: = 1 if result = 0
C = n
V = n

IOCOPY: Copy a value to/from the I/O register. The I/O address can be either argument – but not both.

Execution Time: 1 + argument + 1 + K

The +1 is for reading the I/O address, the +K is for accessing the I/O device.

Length: 2 + argument + 2

The +2 is for the I/O address.

Examples:

```
iocopy.1    R0, SP0DATA       ; copy 1 byte of R0 to Serial Port
                              ; 0 Data Register
                              ; K=1, T=1+0+1+1=3, B=2+0+2=4
```

Timing Details:

1 = read the instruction
0 = access R0
1 = read the I/O address
1 = write 1 byte to the I/O device

```
iocopy.4    T0DATA, (R0)      ; copy 4 bytes from Timer 0 Data
                              ; Register to (R0)
                              ; K=2, T=1+1+2+2=6, B=2+2+0=4
```

Timing Details:

1 = read the instruction
1 = read the I/O address
2 = read 4 bytes from the I/O device
2 = write 4 bytes to the address contained in R0

Condition Codes:

N = x: = value of the result MSB: = 1 if result is negative
Z = x: = 1 if result = 0
C = n
V = n

IOOR: Logically-or the argument with the I/O register. The I/O register is always the second argument – the destination.

This instruction can be used to set bits in I/O registers.

Execution Time: $1 + \text{argument} + 1 + 2 \cdot K + 1$

The first +1 is for reading the I/O address, the +2 ·K is for accessing the I/O device using a read-modify-write cycle, the second +1 is to perform the "or" operation.

Length: $2 + \text{argument} + 2$

The +2 is for the I/O address.

Example:

```
ioor.l     R0, SP0DATA      ; logically-or 1 byte of R0 to
                            ; Serial Port 0 Data Register
                            ; K=1, T=1+0+1+(2*1)+1=5, B=2+0+2=4
```

Timing Details:

1 = read the instruction
0 = access R0
1 = read the I/O address
1 = read 1 byte from the I/O register
1 = perform the "or" operation
1 = write 1 byte to the I/O device

Condition Codes:

N = x: = value of the result MSB: = 1 if result is negative
Z = x: = 1 if result = 0
C = n
V = n

IOTST: Test the state of a single bit in an I/O register. The content of the I/O register is not modified. The instruction will usually be followed by a conditional branch. The bit number is limited to the range 0 to 15 and must always be immediate mode.

This instruction will usually be followed by either the BCS or BCC conditional branch instructions. BEQ or BNE could be used instead but the logic is inverted.

Execution Time: 1 + 1 + K + 1

The first +1 is for reading the I/O address, the +K is for reading the I/O device, the second +1 is to perform an "and" operation.

Length: 2 + argument + 2

The +2 is for the I/O address.

Example:

```
iotst.l    #3, SP0STAT      ; Test bit 3 of Serial Port 0
                            ; Status Register
                            ; K=1, T=1+1+1+1+1=5, B=2+2+2=6
```

Timing Details:

1 = read the instruction – the bit number is embedded in the opcode so it does not require any additional clock cycles to read it.
1 = read the I/O address
1 = read 1 byte from the I/O register
1 = perform the "test" operation

Condition Codes:

N = x: = only affected if the MSB of the I/O register is being tested
Z = x: = 1 if the bit is NOT set
C = x: = 1 if the bit is set
V = n

Block Copy

These instructions copy a block from one location in to another location. Only the Z-bit is affected and will be 1 when the instruction completes. They use specific registers as follows:

R0 = Unsigned number of units to copy
R1 = Source address
R2 = Destination address

The address register(s) get incremented until R0 decrements to 0, as the data is copied; therefore, the instruction can be interrupted. R0 is tested BEFOR the copy operation.

All three registers are modified AFTER each copy operation. Both source and destination can be memory or I/O.

The execution time for the instructions is identical and is calculated as follows:

T = read instruction + (read data (R1) + write data (R2) + update (R0, R1 & R2) for each unit copied).

$$T = 1 + (K + K + 1) \cdot R0 = 1 + (2 \cdot K + 1) \cdot R0$$

Where K is one, two or four based on the specified data size.

The instruction length for the instructions is identical and is two.

BC: All registers get updated as the data is copied.

Example:

```
bc.2                             ; copy R0 words from (R1) to (R2)
                                 ; T=1+(2*1+1)*R0=1+3*R0
```

This is equivalent to:

```
Loop:       ; test for interrupts occurs here
            ; interrupts disabled for the following instructions
copy.2      (R1), (R2)         ; copy the data
incp.2      R1                 ; update source pointer
incp.2      R2                 ; update destination pointer
dbne        R0, Loop           ; update counter and branch if not
                               ; done
```

BCIS: Increment only R1 (source pointer)

Example:

```
bcis.4                           ; copy R0 longwords from (R1) to
                                 ; (R2)
                                 ; T=1+(2*2+1)*R0=1+5*R0
```

This is equivalent to:

```
Loop:       ; test for interrupts occurs here
            ; interrupts disabled for the following instructions
copy.4      (R1), (R2)         ; copy the data
incp.4      R1                 ; update source pointer
dbne        R0, Loop           ; update counter and branch if not
                               ; done
```

BCID: Increment only R2 (destination pointer)

Example:

```
bcid.8                           ; copy R0 quadwords from (R1) to
                                 ; (R2)
                                 ; T=1+(2*3+1)*R0=1+7*R0
```

This is equivalent to:

```
Loop:       ; test for interrupts occurs here
            ; interrupts disabled for the following instructions
copy.8      (R1), (R2)         ; copy the data
incp.8      R2                 ; update destination pointer
dbne        R0, Loop           ; update counter and branch if not done
```

Status Register and Miscellaneous

CCC: Condition Code Clear

CCS: Condition Code Set

These two instructions allow you to explicitly control the state of the conditions codes. The only condition code bit that is affected is the one specified by the instruction. The assembler names for the conditions codes are:

NBIT, ZBIT, CBIT and VBIT

Examples:

```
ccc     CBIT          ; clear the C-bit; T=1, B=2
ccs     CBIT          ; set the C-bit
```

Note that only a single bit can be specified as the argument.

PSRCOPY: Copy the PSR to the specified destination. This instruction does not affect the condition codes. Note that the PSR is 2 bytes. All destination modes are allowed.

Execution Time: 1 + argument

Length: 2 + argument

Example:

```
psrcopy    R0              ; copy the PSR to R0
                           ; T=1+0, B=2+0=2
```

SETIPL: Set the Interrupt Priority Level.

Example:

```
setipl     0               ; set the IPL to 0
                           ; T=1, B=2
```

NOP: no operation. This is essentially a dummy instruction that does absolutely nothing except take 1 clock and 2 bytes. Sometimes this instruction is used in a timing loop where the number of clocks is being tailored for a specific count.

Example:

```
nop                              ; T=1, B=2
```

An interesting point about the NOP instruction is that its opcode is sometimes chosen based on the type of memory from which instructions will be executed. Most flash devices will have 0xFF in all erased locations so it might be reasonable to have the NOP instruction be 0xFFFF. In some devices, it might be better to use 0x0000.

Other possibilities of instructions whose opcodes might be tailored to specific memory devices could be HALT or even Branch-to-Self. Either of these would allow a Watch Dog Timer to time out and restart the program.

It might be worthwhile to have both 0x0000 and 0xFFFF be used as opcodes for the same instruction.

WFI: Wait for Interrupt. This instruction can be used where fast response to interrupts is needed. The instruction pushes the PC and PSR onto the stack, suspends execution of any further instructions and waits for an interrupt. Now the interrupt can be handled more quickly than normal because the CPU does not have to finish processing the current instruction nor does it have to push the PC and PSR onto the stack.

Example:

```
wfi                              ; T + 2 (new PSR based on new IPL,
                                 ; retrieve ISR address from the
                                 ; interrupt vector)
                                 ; B = 2
```

9
A Few Algorithms

Duplicate Instructions?

As you reviewed the instruction set, you may have asked yourself "Why is this instruction here since the same results can be obtained using another instruction?" In general, the answer is because "this" instruction is faster and probably takes less memory. Processor designers try to determine what instructions will yield the most efficient code for the target applications. The following are a few examples.

The CLR instruction writes a value of 0 to the destination operand. This can also be accomplished by using the COPY instruction with an argument one value of 0. Using a register as the destination, the CLR instruction will take 1 clock cycle and be 2 bytes, independent of the operand size. The COPY instruction is dependent on the operand size and will take 2, 3 or 5 clock cycles and be 4, 6 or 10 bytes.

The INCrement and DECrement instructions are justified in exactly the same way. The INCP and DECP instructions are more efficient than the equivalent ADD and SUB instructions when stepping through blocks of values.

Multiply and Divide

Some processors do not have integer multiply and/or divide instructions. If not, they must have some means of performing these operations via any of several algorithms. This short discussion deals only with the simplest implementations. Faster algorithms will be more complex as well as more difficult to explain. You can find some of these on the Internet simply by searching for "divide and multiply algorithm."

This section discusses only integer algorithms, attempting floating point is quite beyond the scope of this book.

These multiplication and division algorithms only work when both values are positive. Here is some code in C which can be used to allow them to handle any combination of signs:

```
NegateFlag = 0;
if ( Valuel < 0 ) { Valuel = - Valuel; NegateFlag = 1; }
if ( Value2 < 0 ) { Value2 = - Value2; NegateFlag += 1; }
```

Now both values will be positive. After executing the desired algorithm, all you need to do is test NegateFlag:

```
if ( NegateFlag = 1 ) Result = -Result; // change sign if
                              // original values had different signs
```

Multiplication Algorithms

The easiest method of multiplying two integers (2 bytes each) is to add a value, the multiplicand, to itself the required number of times, the multiplier, as shown in this example using the C language to calculate C = A · B:

```
int A, B;
long C;
C = 0;
while ( B ) { C += A; B--;}
```

In BASIC, it would look something like:

```
C = 0
WHILE ( B 0 )
   C = C + A
   B = B - 1
WEND
```

As you can see from both of these, the larger the value of B the longer the calculation will take. More complex algorithms use shifting and have basically one small set of calculations per bit so the multiplication time is dependent only on the size of the operands and the number of ones in the multiplier.

You should note that in higher level languages you do not generally have to be concerned with the number of bytes in the intermediate values. Since the multiplicand is added to the result it should be the same size. However, both BASIC and C will promote the multiplicand to 32 bits in order to add them. This is certainly not the case in assembly language – you have to do the promotion yourself as is shown in the last two examples.

Another method which is used in hardware multipliers is sometimes called the *shift and add* method. It performs successive shifts of the multiplicand adding the shifted value to the result only if the corresponding bit of the multiplier is set. Since this algorithm shifts the Multiplicand, it needs to be defined as long (4 bytes) to ensure that an overflow does not occur. Here is what it would look like in C for multiplying 16 bit values, again assuming both values are positive:

```
int Multiplier, i;
long Result, Multiplicand;

Result = 0;
Multiplicand = 56;
Multiplier = 38;

for (i=0; i<16; i++ )
{
   if ( Multiplier & 1 )  Result += Multiplicand;
   Multiplicand <<= 1;
   Multiplier >>= 1;
}
```

This can be made a little more efficient if the loop is exited when the Multiplier become 0. Here is a step by step example showing $56 \cdot 38$:

Fig. 9.1

Iteration	Multiplicand	Multiplier	Multiplier & 1	Result
1	56	38	0	0
2	112	19	1	112
3	224	9	1	336
4	448	4	0	336
5	896	2	0	336
6	1792	1	1	2128
7	3584	0	0	2128

Here is what the code would look like using the assembly language for this processor using dedicated locations in RAM for the values:

```
; Example_Multiplier.asm

#address        NEXT_RAM     ; set up to allocate the variables
Result:         alloc.4
Multiplicand:   #alloc.4
Multiplier:     #alloc.2

#address        NEXT_PC 0x1000  ; set the PC for the code
#vector         VECTOR_START    ; to eliminate assembler error
#vector         VECTOR_RTC      ;   "    "    "    "
#address        NEXT_PC      ; set the PC for the code
```

```
    clr.4         Result        ; initialize the result and the
                                ; values to multiply
    copy.4        #0d56, Multiplicand    ; make 4 bytes because
                                         ; the Multiplicand is
                                         ; added to the Result
    copy.2        #0d38, Multiplier
Mpy_Loop:
    bitest.1      #1, Multiplicand       ; check for bit 0 set
    beq           Do_not_add             ; branch if bit 0 not
                                         ; set
    add.4         Multiplicand, Result   ; update the result
Do_not_add:
    sla.4         Multiplicand           ; update
    srl.2         Multiplier             ; values
    bne           Mpy_Loop      ; branch if Multiplier not 0

; Result now contains the product of the two values
```

Please notice a few things about this code:

It does not count the number of iterations – this is because the Multiplier will become 0 within the iteration count due to the way the SRL instruction works.

Both the Result and Multiplicand are allocated double the size that is required to contain the original values. This is necessary because:

Multiplying 16 bit values can easily yield a 32 bit result

The Multiplicand is successively shifted left which can also generate a 32 bit value

There are no registers used – this is somewhat inefficient.

The following example shows the same algorithm using registers.

```
    clr.4         r0            ; initialize the result and the
                                ; values to multiply
    copy.4        #0d56, r1     ; initialize Multiplicand
    copy.2        #0d38, r2     ; initialize Multiplier
Mpy_LoopA:
    srlc.2        r2            ; shift the Multiplier getting bit
                                ; 0 into the C-bit
    bcc           Do_not_addA   ; branch if C-bit is clear
    add.4         r1, r0        ; update the result
```

```
Do_not_addA:
    sla.4         r1           ; update Multiplicand
    test.2        r2           ; check if done
    bne           Mpy_LoopA    ; branch if Multiplier not 0

; r0 now contains the product of the two values
```

This routine will execute at least twice as fast as the previous one because it is completely register based. Note that the code can be easily extended to multiply 8 bit and 32 bit values as well simply by changing the size values in each of the instructions to **.8** instead of **.4**. A slightly more complex function could be written in order to support 64 bit values as well.

Division Algorithms

The easiest method of integer division uses successive subtractions of the divisor from the dividend, as shown in this example using the C language to calculate C = A/B:

```
int A, B, C;
A = 12343;
B = 5;
C = 0;
while ( A>B ) {A = A-B; C++; }
// C = quotient, A = remainder
```

In BASIC, it would look something like:

```
C = 0
WHILE A>B
    A = A-B
    C = C+1
WEND
```

It should be obvious from this algorithm that the quotient is also the number of times the loop is executed.

A more efficient algorithm is somewhat similar to the multiplication *shift and add* but uses a *shift and subtract* method. This is a bit harder because the first step is to "align" the MSB of divisor with that of the dividend. Another complicating factor is that a mask consisting of the number of bits in the divisor must be generated. The following two loops in C perform this task for a 16 bit divide:

```
int Dividend, Divisor, Quotient;
int i, Mask, ShiftCount;
```

```
Dividend = 1234;
Divisor = 27;
i = 0x8000;        // set the MSB to find the highest bit in the
                   // dividend
while ( !(i & Dividend) ) i = (i>>1) ;     // shift i until the
                                           // MSB in Dividend is found
           // as the bit in i is shifted to the right, it will
           // eventually be in the same position as the MSB of
           // Dividend

/* Now shift the divisor until its MSB aligns with i. As the bits in
Divisor are shifted left, the MSB will eventually align with the MSB
of Dividend. The Mask will shift with the Divisor but a 0 bit will
be inserted into LSB position with each shift.  Update ShiftCount
with each shift. */
   Mask = -1;          // initialize the Mask to all 1's
   ShiftCount = 1;     // initialize the number of shifts
   while ( !(i & Divisor) ) { Divisor <<= 1; Mask <<= 1;
   ShiftCount += 1;}
// Now the MSBs of the Dividend and the Divisor are aligned.
// The Mask contains 1's in the bits used by the Divisor (as
// well as the higher bits - which do not matter).

   Quotient = 0;       // initialize the quotient
// now perform the shift and subtract for each shift performed
// in shifting the divisor.
   do
   {
      Quotient <<= 1;              // Quotient is always shifted
      if ( (Dividend & Mask) >= Divisor)  // only compare the
                                   // bits of Dividend that are
                                   // "covered" by the mask
      {   Dividend = Dividend-Divisor;    // do the "subtract"
          Quotient |= 1;                  // insert the 1
      }
      Divisor >>= 1;
      Mask >>= 1;
      ShiftCount -= 1;
   } while (ShiftCount);
// The Quotient now contains the correct value and the
// Dividend contains the remainder.
}
```

The following table shows the details of dividing 1234 by 27 *after* shifting the divisor (27) to line it up with the MSB of the dividend and determining the mask and shift count values. Note that the mask contains 5 bits – the number of bits required to represent the divisor. Each line of the table is one iteration of the loop.

Fig. 9.2

Dividend 1234	Mask	Dividend & Mask	Divisor 27 << 6	Shift Count	Quotient
100 1101 0010	111 1100 0000	100 1100 0000	110 1100 0000	7	0
100 1101 0010	111 1110 0000	100 1100 0000	011 0110 0000	6	1
001 0111 0010	111 1111 0000	001 0111 0000	001 1011 0000	5	10
001 0111 0010	111 1111 1000	001 0111 0000	000 1101 1000	4	101
000 1001 1010	111 1111 1100	000 1001 1000	000 0110 1100	3	1011
000 0010 1110	111 1111 1110	000 0010 1110	000 0011 0110	2	10110
000 0010 1110	111 1111 1111	000 0010 1110	000 0001 1011	1	101101
000 0001 0011	–	–	–	0	

The following is what it would look like using assembly language of this processor. The algorithm will use a combination of memory locations and registers.

```
;Example_Divider.asm

#nprint     PR_PROC_DEFS    ; do not print the processor
                            ; definitions

#address    NEXT_RAM 0x100000    ; set up to allocate the
                                 ; variables
Dividend:   #alloc.2
Divisor:    #alloc.2
Quotient:   #alloc.2

#address    NEXT_PC 0x1000       ; set the PC for the code
#vector     VECTOR_START         ; to eliminate assembler error
#vector     VECTOR_RTC           ;   "    "    "     "

   copy.2     #1234, Dividend    ; initialize the
   copy.2     #27, Divisor       ; two values
   clr.2      Quotient           ; initialize the quotient
   comp.2     Divisor, Dividend  ; is Divisor > Dividend?
   bgt        DivideExit         ; branch if yes
   clr        R0                 ; set up
   ccs        cbit               ; mask for finding MSB of
                                 ; Dividend
Loop_1:
   rrc        R0                 ; put mask into next lower bit
   bitest.2   R0, Dividend       ; found MSB yet?
   beq        Loop_1             ; branch if no
```

```
; R0 now contains a single bit which is in the MSB position of
; the Dividend
   copy.2    #-1, R1            ; initialize mask
   copy.2    #1, R2             ; initialize shift counter
Loop_2:
   bitest.2  R0, Divisor        ; found MSB of Divisor?
   bne       Label_1            ; branch if yes
   inc.2     R2                 ; update shift counter
   sla.2     R1                 ; update mask
   sla.2     Divisor            ; shift divisor
   br        Loop_2             ; until done
; now MSB of divisor is in same bit position as MSB of
; Dividen
; R2 = shift counter  R1 = mask ( a '1' in each bit used by
; the Divisor )
Label_1:
   sla.2     Quotient           ; Quotient always gets shifted
   copy.2    Dividend, R0       ; get working copy of Dividend
   and.2     R1, R0             ; R0 = Dividend & Mask
   comp.2    R0, Divisor        ; is (Dividend & Mask) >=
                                ; Divisor?
   blt       Label_2            ; branch if no
   sub.2     Divisor, Dividend  ; Dividend = Dividend - Divisor
   or.2      #1, Quotient       ; insert 1 into quotient
Label_2:
   sra.2     Divisor            ; update divisor
   sra.2     R1                 ; update mask
   dbne      R2, Label_1        ; update shift counter and
                                ; branch if not done
DivideExit:

; Quotient now contains the correct value and Dividend
; contains the remainder.
```

These division algorithms might seem a little complicated as well as looking like they might take quite a while to execute. However, the shift and subtract method will generally take less time than a loop that subtracts the Divisor from the Dividend many times. Some processors have another assembly language instruction which would make the algorithm more efficient – locate the MSB of the operand. This instruction would remove the necessity for the first two loops. The code would look something like this:

```
   fmsb.2    Dividend, R2       ; R2 = MSB position of Dividend
   fmsb.2    Divisor, R1        ; R1 = MSB position of Divisor
   sub.2     R1, R2             ; R2 = R2 - R1 = nbr of times
```

```
                                ; Divisor needs to be shifted
                                ; to line up the MSBs
        ashift.2  R2, Divisor   ; shift the divisor to line up
                                ; the MSBs
```

The mask and shift counter still have to be developed and can be done like this:

```
        copy.2    #-1, R1       ; initialize the mask
        ashift.2  R2, R1        ; shift the mask to line up
                                ; with the Divisor
        inc.2     R2            ; R2 = shift count
```

These few examples should give you a good idea of the methodology used to develop "higher level" instruction alternatives for those processors that do not implement them in hardware.

10
Simple Exercises

Here are a few simple exercises just to get you introduced to programming in Assembly language.

Exercise 1

Task: Generate the fastest possible square wave out of one of the parallel ports – do not use a **P**ulse **M**odulator. Use a technique often referred to as "bit banging".

This is a very simple task which should only take a few instructions. However, there will still need to be a minimum amount of set up – mostly definitions – in order to write even the simplest program. Here is a brief outline of the initialization. This will be mostly the same for almost any program written for this processor:

1. Define the memory configuration values
2. Define any other constants that may be needed for this task
   a) Serial port values
   b) Other values
3. Interrupt Vectors
4. Any required constants
5. Any required RAM
   a) Pointers
   b) Buffers
   c) Counters
6. Program code

This is a detailed description of the initialization required. Future samples/exercises will need essentially the same set up so the same code will be shown but without the explanatory comments. Only additions and changes will be explained. You will also notice comment lines which are full of '*'s. This is my way of indicating a major portion of code or the start of a function. Doing this makes is visually easier to see new blocks of code when scanning the source.

```
; Exercise 1
/********************* Memory Definitions ***********************
These first values define the memory configuration and the memory
definitions for the Address Pointer. The memory definitions are
completely dependent on the memory devices connected to the processor,
how they are connected and how the processor configures their control
signals when it comes out of reset. The assumption here is that the
flash (program memory) starts at address 0. For many processors this
is a valid assumption. However, the starting address of RAM may have
to be set up by the initialization code. Here we are assuming that
this is not the case and that RAM starts at address 0x40000.
*/

;         define the RAM values
#define   RAMSTART   0x40000    ; starting address of RAM
#define   RAMSIZE    0x40000    ; and its size
#define   RAMEND     RAMSTART + RAMSIZE
                                ; calculate the end address of the RAM

;         define the stack size and location
#define   STACKSIZE  0x1000              ; size of stack
#define   STACK_TOP  RAMEND - STACKSIZE  ; top of the stack

;         define the values for the Address Pointer
#address  NEXT_ROM   0x0400     ; starting address to put any
                                ; constants
#address  NEXT_PC    0x1000     ; starting address of the program
#address  NEXT_RAM   RAMSTART   ; start of the RAM

;*************************************************************
; Define any other values that may be needed for this task
; ***     Other values

;*************************************************************
; Any required constants

#address  NEXT_ROM
```

```
; there are none for this example

;*************************************************************
; Any required RAM

#address  NEXT_RAM               ; set the Address Pointer to the
                                 ; next available RAM
; no RAM is required for this example

;*************************************************************
; Code

/* Remember that the assembler will generate an error if NEXT_ROM
attempts to use memory beyond the initial value of NEXT_PC. If this
does happen, all that is needed is to redefine the initial value of
NEXT_PC. If you want to automatically set the value of NEXT_PC to be
just past the constants, all you need to do is NOT define NEXT_PC
where the other NEXT_... values are and do the following instead:

          #address   NEXT_PC    NEXT_ROM

However, this method then disallows you from using NEXT_ROM from this
point forward.
*/

#address  NEXT_PC                ; set the Address Pointer to the start
                                 ; of the program

#vector   VECTOR_RTC             ; dummy ISR required by the assembler
 reti

#vector   VECTOR_START           ; set the start up vector to point to
                                 ; the first instruction

;**************** begin program code ***************************

Main:                            ; a name is not really needed here
; Even though interrupts are not needed in this sample, nor are any
; functions called, the Stack Pointer should still be initialized.
   copy.4        #RAMTOP, SP     ; set stack pointer to top of RAM -
                                 ; bottom of the stack

/* The first thing to do is enable a parallel port bit to be an
output. Which one? For this exercise we will use Port 2 bit 4. The
```

```
selection of PP2.4 is somewhat arbitrary – basically I just did not
want to use PP0.0.
*/

/* Note: The assembler has a set of pre-defined values for each of the
bits from 0 to 31: BIT00, ... BIT31 You can find these definitions in
Processor_Definitions.h.
*/

   iocopy.l        #1, PP2.4CFG   ; set PP2.4 as an output to use
                                  ; PP2DATA
Main_1:                           ; need a label for the loop
   ioor.l          #BIT04, PP2DATA    ; 6 bit 4 = 1
   ioand.l         #~BIT04, PP2DATA   ; 6 bit 4 = 0
   br              Main_1             ; 3
          ; total loop time = 15 clocks: duty cycle = 6/15 = 40%

/* That's all there is to it! However, this is not a 50% duty cycle
due to the execution time of the br instruction.

In case you are wondering about the construction: ~BIT04, the "~" is a
unary operator which means "1's complement" – it inverts all the bits.
In this case the value BIT04 was defined as 0x0010, so ~BIT4 = 0xFFEF.
However, since the data size is defined as one, the representation in
the .LST file will show the value as 00EF since byte values are shown
as words (2 bytes). The CPU would use only the low byte of the value
when executing the instruction.

The following set of instructions will make it 50% using the same I/O
registers.
*/

   iocopy.l        #1, PP2.4CFG   ; set PP2.4 as an output to use
                                  ; PP2DATA
Main_2:                           ; need a label for the loop
   ioor.l          #BIT04, PP2DATA    ; 6 bit 4= 1
   br              Main_3             ; 3 cause a 3 clock delay
Main_3:
   ioand.l         #~BIT04, PP2DATA   ; 6 bit 4 = 0
   br              Main_2             ; 3
          ; total loop time = 18 clocks: duty cycle = 9/18 = 50%

; Here is another solution – one that uses only PP2.4CFG by varying
; the state of bit 3
```

```
   iocopy.1       #2, PP2.4CFG  ; set PP2.4 to use bit 3 for its state
Main_4:                         ; need a label for the loop
   iocopy.1       #2|BIT03, PP2.4CFG   ; 4 bit 4 = 1
   br             Main_5        ; 3 cause a 3 clock delay
Main_5:
   iocopy.1       #2, PP2.4CFG  ; 4 bit 4 = 0
   br             Main_4        ; 3
          ; total loop time = 14 clocks: duty cycle = 7/14 = 50%
```

/* In the previous two examples, the added **br** instruction could be replaced with any dummy instruction that takes 3 clocks but using the **br** makes it a lot more obvious that the 1 and 0 times will be the same.
Note that the above are not the only solutions. Here is another possibility – also almost the fastest:
*/

```
   copy.4         #PP2.4CFG, r0 ; r0 = address of the I/O register
Main_6:                         ; need a label for the loop
   copy.1         #2|BIT03, (r0)   ; 3 bit 4 = 1
   copy.1         #2, (r0)      ; 3 bit 4 = 0
   br             Main_6        ; 3
          ; total loop time = 9 clocks: duty cycle = 3/9 = 33%
```

/*Note that the loop contains "normal" copy instructions. This is because the *iocopy* instruction requires an I/O address as one of its arguments. Using (r0) is not an I/O address.
This will execute faster because the address of the I/O register does not have to be read from the instructions. Since this set of instructions does not have the "extra" **br** instruction it will also not be a 50% duty cycle. With these instructions the imbalance in the 1 and 0 times will be more evident while the frequency will be higher. The reason for the more obvious imbalance is due to the 3 clocks of the **br** instruction being a higher percentage of the total loop time.

What has been shown with these four examples that do essentially the same task is that there are usually several solutions to almost every programming task. What they also attempt to show is that to be most efficient in assembly language you have to know the hardware of the processor. The better you know the hardware, the better will be your solution.

Note that by using two more registers the loop time can be decreased to seven clocks – this would be the fastest.
*/

Exercise 2

```
/*Task: Generate a very low frequency square wave out of one of the
parallel port bits using "bit banging."
Now lets make the previous program a little more complicated – insert
a delay in both the "1" and "0" times using the simplest possible
method. Since there is no delay function, what is a simple way of gen-
erating a delay? We implemented one in the second solution above by
adding a "dummy" instruction. We can extend this method quite easily
as shown below.
Note: this example does not show all of the initialization statements
– it gets right into the program code.
*/

Main:
   copy.4       #RAMEND, SP    ; set stack pointer to top of RAM  -
                               ; bottom of the stack
   iocopy.1     #1, PP2.4CFG   ; set PP2.3 as an output to use
                               ; PP3DATA
   clr.2        r0             ; set r0 = 0 for loop counter
Main_1:                        ; need a label for the loop
   dbne         r0, Main_1     ; decrement r0 until it reaches 0
   or.1         #BIT04, PP2DATA    ; bit 4 = 1
                                   ; note that R0 = 0
Main_2:
   dbne         r0, Main_2         ; decrement r0 until it reaches 0
   and.1        #~BIT04, PP2DATA   ; bit 4 = 0
   br           Main_1             ; start the pulse over
```

/* Note that the delay precedes the change in the output state. This will generate a square wave with a very long period! Each state will be several clocks longer than (65535 * 3) clocks. The 65535 is because the first value in r0 that the **dbne** instructions get is 0. The test for 0 is done after the decrement. The reason it is not 65536 is that on the last iteration the branch will not be taken, when r0 = 0. The factor of 3 is because every branch instruction takes 3 clock cycles if the branch is taken. Note that the execution time of the actual output statements is not included in the calculations – this is because they are negligible relative to the **dbne** time. The degree of asymmetry will be about three parts in 6 * 66535 and is due to the last **br** instruction. If 100% symmetry is required, 3 clock cycles of dummy instructions can be inserted immediately preceding Main_2. If the processor has a 100 MHz clock each state will be quite close to 1.966 msec yielding a square wave of about 254 Hz.

```
It should be noted that a really easy way to generate an even lower
frequency square wave is to insert one or more "dummy" instructions
between the dbne instructions and their target br locations.
*/
```

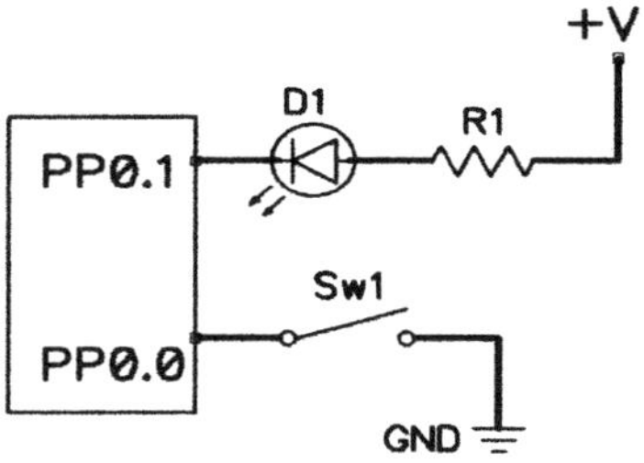

Fig. 10.1

Exercise 3

```
/*Task: Make an LED follow the state of a switch.

This example reads the state of an input and sets an output to the
same state. If the input is connected to a switch and the output
drives an LED then the on/off state of the LED is controlled by the
state of the switch. The switch will be connected between the parallel
port bit and ground; therefore, the bit needs a pullup. The LED will
be connected between the port bit and +V through an appropriate
current limiting resistor; therefore, the bit needs to be able to sink
enough current to light the LED. Figure 10.1 shows the schematic.
*/

;********************** Memory Definitions ************************
;          define the RAM values
#define    RAMSTART   0x40000     ; starting address of RAM
#define    RAMSIZE    0x40000     ; and its size
#define    RAMEND     RAMSTART+ RAMSIZE  ; calculate the end address of
                                         ; the RAM

;          define the stack size and location
#define    STACKSIZE  0x1000      ; size of stack
#define    STACK_TOP  RAMEND - STACKSIZE ; top of the stack

;          define the values for the Address Pointer
#address   NEXT_ROM   0x400       ; starting address to put any
                                  ; constants
#address   NEXT_PC    0x1000      ; starting address of the program
```

```
#address   NEXT_RAM   RAMSTART    ; start of the RAM

;          defines for the states of the LED
#define    LED_ON     0x52        ; open drain, 8ma,
                                  ; output = 0 - turns LED on
#define    LED_OFF    0x52|BIT03  ; open drain, 8ma,
                                  ; output = 1 - turns LED off

#address   NEXT_PC                ; set the Address Pointer to the start
                                  ; of the program
#vector    VECTOR_START           ; set the start up vector to point to
                                  ; the first instruction

;*************** begin program code ****************************

Main:
   copy.4        #RAMEND, SP      ; set stack pointer to top of RAM -
                                  ; bottom of the stack

;          set up the 2 I/O ports
   iocopy.1      #0x90, PP0.0CFG     ; PP0.0 = input, 20K load, pullup
   iocopy.1      #LED_OFF, PP0.1CFG ; PP0.1 = LED off

Main_1:
   iocopy.1      PP0DATA, r0      ; read PP0
   rrc.1         r0               ; bit 0 ==> C-bit
   bcc           Main_2           ; br if the switch is closed -
                                  ; grounded

;          here if the switch is open
   iocopy.1      #LED_OFF, PP0.1CFG   ; PP0.1 = LED off
   br            Main_1

;          here if the switch is closed
Main_2:
   iocopy.1      #LED_ON, PP0.1CFG    ; PP0.1 = LED on
   br            Main_1               ; start over
```

/* Just as in the previous examples, there is more than one set of statements that will do the same thing. The only way to make it more efficient would be to put the addresses of **PP0DATA** and **PP0.1CFG** into registers. This would save six bytes of code memory and 3 clock cycles within the loop but would add six bytes and eight clock cycles to the setup.

```
Another important criteria that may not be very obvious is the reason
for selecting the I/O bits as defined. Bit 0 was selected for the
switch input simply because detecting the switch state requires only
reading the register and doing a single shift. Another method is as
follows:

   iocopy.l          PP0DATA, r0   ; read PP0
   and.l             #BIT00, r0    ; leave only bit 0
   beq               SomeAddr      ; br if bit is a 0 – switch is
                                   ; closed

This set of instructions is more general purpose in that it will work
for any bit as long as the mask is defined correctly, but it does take
an extra byte.

And yet another partial solution:

   bitest.l          #BIT00, PP0DATA   ; is switch closed?
   beq               SomeAddr          ; br if yes
*/
```

Exercise 4

```
/* Exercise_4.asm
   Task Description
Task: Create a Pulse Modulated signal of 1KHz with a 25% duty cycle.
The CPU frequency is not fixed, it is stored in a processor register
named CPU_FREQUENCY with 1 Hz resolution.

The program will need to do some calculations in order to determine
the divisor values for the Timer and PM registers.
*/

;********************** Memory Definitions *********************
;           define the RAM values
#define     RAMSTART    0x40000              ; starting address of RAM
#define     RAMSIZE     0x40000              ; and its size
#define     RAMEND      RAMSTART+ RAMSIZE    ; calculate the end address
                                             ; of the RAM

;           define the stack size and location
#define     STACKSIZE   0x1000               ; size of stack
#define     STACK_TOP   RAMEND - STACKSIZE   ; top of the stack
```

```
;         define the values for the Address Pointer
#address  NEXT_ROM   0x400              ; starting address to put any
                                        ; constants
#address  NEXT_PC    0x1000             ; starting address of the
                                        ; program
#address  NEXT_RAM   RAMSTART           ; start of the RAM
;*************************************************************

#address  NEXT_PC               ; set the Address Pointer to the start
                                ; of the program
#vector   VECTOR_START          ; set the start up vector to point to
                                ; the first instruction

;********************** begin program code *********************

Main:
   copy.4        #RAMEND, SP    ; set stack pointer to top of RAM -
                                ; bottom of the stack

/* Use Timer 0 as the time base for the PM signal and PP2.3 as the
output pin. Calculate the divisor needed to produce a 1ms period. Set
the appropriate registers to generate a continuous pulse stream. Due
to the processor configuration of the PM signals, it is necessary to
use PM3 – see Sample Port Assignments at the end of Chapter 5.
Additional comments indicate the details of the hardware registers
being programmed.
*/

;         calculate the T0 divisor – dividing the CPU frequency by the
;         desired frequency will yield the required divisor value
   copy.4        CPU_FREQUENCY, r0      ; get the CPU frequency
   div.4         #1000, r0              ; r0 = PM divisor

;         set up the T0 registers
   iocopy.4      r0, T0DATA     ; set the T0 divisor
   clr.1         T0CLK          ; T0 clock source = internal
   iocopy.1      #0xC0, T0CFG   ; start counting, max count = T0DATA,
                                ; pre-scale divisor = 1
                                ; bit 7 = 1 = 0x80 = enable timer
                                ; bit 6 = 1 = 0x40 = use T0DATA as max
                                ; count
                                ; bit 4 = 0 = free run
                                ; bits 2,1,0 = 0 = pre-scale divisor
                                ; = 1
```

```
   iocopy.l        #0x87, PP2.3CFG  ; PP2.3 = fast edge, 4ma, CMOS, PM3
                                    ; bit 7 = 1 = 0x80 = Fast edge
                                    ; bit 6 = 0 = CMOS
                                    ; bits 5,4 = 0 = 4ma drive
                                    ; bits 2,1,0 = 7 = PM3
;          set up the PM registers
   iocopy.l        #0x80, PM3CFG    ; PWM, Timer 0, no interrupt
                                    ; bit 7 = 1 = 0x80 = Enable PWM
                                    ; bits 6,5,4 = 0 = use Timer 0
                                    ; bits 2,1,0 = 0 = no interrupt

;          to get the on time, divide the period count by 4
   div.4           #4, r0         ; on time = period/4
   iocopy.4        r0, PM3WIDTH   ; set PWM on time

;          there should now be pulses on PP2.3

Main_l:
   br              Main_l         ; forever loop

#vector   VECTOR_RTC              ; dummy ISR required by the assembler
  reti
```

11
Interrupt Service Routines

Interrupts allow the program to respond quickly to predefined, asynchronous events. The source of those events can be either internal to the processor or external. See *This Processor – Interrupts* for more details.

An Interrupt Service Routine is simply a special case of a function/subroutine that is executed when the interrupt is acknowledged by the processor.

Here are a few rules and suggestions for writing ISRs:

- Rules
  - Keep them as short as possible – do the minimum necessary
  - Save all registers that are used and restore them, usually in the reverse order as saving them, on exiting
  - Use the lowest IPL that will accomplish the task
  - Be sure to clear the interrupt! This may seem obvious, but some interrupts are cleared by reading from or writing to a register which may not otherwise need to be accessed by the ISR.
- Suggestions
  - Use Assembly language
  - Do NOT use looping constructions
  - Do NOT call functions/subroutines
  - Put the number of clock cycles for each instruction in the comments

The following sample ISRs are for Serial Port 0 receive and transmit. You will notice that there are no references to the parallel port registers that are associated with the serial port. That is because some initialization code had to have been executed that set **SP0RPORT** and **PPx.yCFG** to use the appropriate parallel port(s) and bit(s) for serial port 0. In general, the receive and transmit bits will usually be on the same parallel port but it is not necessary.

Serial Port Receive

Below are four sample ISRs that do exactly the same thing – receive a character from an asynchronous serial port and store it into a RAM buffer. They are all commented well and should be fairly easy to follow. However, before we get into the code, here is a review of what needs to be done in the ISR:

- Save the registers as required
- Clear the interrupt
- Read the byte
- Store the byte
- Update the byte count and buffer pointer as required
- Restore the registers
- Return from the interrupt

The amount of code to implement the above outline will vary with the processor architecture and the instruction set. It is good programming practice to outline, or write in pseudo-code, the steps required to implement the function before writing a single line of code.

Depending on the complexity of the function, the outline can become comments within the code. The examples here use this technique.

Here are a few suggestions based on experience:

- Document your code as you write it – saying you will do it later means that it will probably not get done.

- Make your comments meaningful based on the task being performed.

  - Example of bad comment:

```
copy.4  SP0RxBufferAddr, r0   ; copy SP0RxBufferAddr into r0
```

This comment adds no information at all. It simply states in English what the instruction does.

Example of good comment

```
copy.4  SP0RxBufferAddr, r0  ; get the address of the
                             ; buffer pointer
```

Label each functional block of code with a comment describing what it is doing. This will make it much easier to debug.

When referring to processor I/O device registers you should use the pre-defined symbolic names. Please DO NOT look up their addresses and use them in the instructions.

It is usually a good idea to not use hard coded numbers. When numbers are required, it is recommended that you #define a meaningful symbol for the value. The symbol RXIPL_MASK in the samples below is an example.

Sample 1 uses a technique that should work with most processors. It saves and restores the registers which are used.

```
SP0RxISR:   ; serial port 0 Rx Interrupt Service Routine
; save the registers – note that the operand is a mask - one bit per
; register
   pushr.4     1                   ; B=2, T=4 save R0 - the only
                                   ; register used in the ISR

; get the address to store the byte
   copy.4      SP0RxBufferAddr, r0 ; B=6, T=5 get the buffer pointer

; clear the interrupt, read and store the byte
   iocopy.1    SP0DATA, (r0)       ; B=4, T=4 read and store the byte
                                   ; - also clears the interrupt

; update the buffer pointer
   incp.1      r0                  ; B=2, T=2 point to next byte
                                   ; location
   copy.4      r0, SP0RxBufferAddr ; B=6, T=5 save it

; the following instruction could replace the previous two except that
; it takes 1 more clock even though it is 2 less bytes. Incrementing a
; register is much faster than incrementing a pointer in memory.
;  incp.1      SP0RxBufferAddr     ; B=6, T=8

; update the byte count – a 2 byte value
   dec.2       SP0RxByteCount      ; B=6, T=6
```

```
                                       ; T=26 to this point
; disable the interrupt if done
   bne          SP0RxISRexit           ; B=2, T=3/2 branch if not done
                                       ; receiving all bytes
   and.l        #~RXIPL_MASK, SPOINT     ; B=8, T=7 disable the
                                         ; interrupt

; restore the registers and exit the ISR
SP0RxISRexit:
   popr.4       1                      ; B=2, T=4
   reti                                ; B=2, T=6 return from the
                                       ; interrupt

; nbr of instructions = 10             total length = 40 bytes
; total time = 39/45 clocks
; the two numbers for the time are due to the bne instruction - most
; of the time the branch will be executed.
```

Sample 2 performs the same task as Sample 1 but for a different processor – a Rabbit™ 5000. This processor has an enhanced instruction set based on the 8086 and Z180.

> *Note: the HL register pair is in uppercase because, depending on the font, a lower case L (l) looks too much like the digit "1" or uppercase letter "I".*

> *IMPORTANT: The compiler (Dynamic C™) for the Rabbit™ uses different notation for both Immediate and Absolute Address modes than what has been defined for the assembler used for this book. Immediate mode does NOT use a special prefix and Address Absolute mode requires parentheses.*

```
SBRxISR:        ; serial port B Rx Interrupt Service Routine
; save the registers
   push         af                     ; B=1, T=11 save the registers
                                       ; being used
   push         HL                     ; B=1, T=11
                                       ; B=2, T=22
; get and store the byte
   ioi          ld   a, (SBDR)         ; B=4, T=11 read the byte and
                                       ; clear the interrupt
   ld           HL, (SP0RxBufferAddr)    ; B=3, T=11 get pointer to the
                                         ; buffer
   ld           (HL), a                ; B=1, T=6 save the byte
   inc          HL                     ; B=1, T=2 update pointer
; note: the function cannot use inc (HL) because it operates on a
; byte - not a word value
```

```
   ld          (SP0RxBufferAddr), HL    ; B=3, T=13 save updated
                                        ; pointer+
                                        ; B=12, T=43
; update byte count
   ld          HL, (SP0RxByteCount)     ; B=3, T=11 get byte count
   dec         HL                       ; B=1, T=2 update
; note: the function cannot use dec (HL) because it operates on a
; byte - not a word value
   ld          (SP0RxByteCount), HL     ; B=3, T=13 save new byte count
   test        HL                       ; B=1, T=2 check if done all
                                        ; bytes
; note: neither the dec nor ld instruction affects the condition codes
   jr          nz, SP0RxISR_1       ; B=2, T=6 jump if not done
                                    ; B=10, T=34
; disable interrupts on the serial port
   ld          a, (SBCRShadow)      ; B=3, T=9 get the current value
                                    ; of the control register
   and         ~0x03                ; B=2, T=4
                                    ; set IPL for serial port to 0
   ld          (SBCRShadow), a      ; B=3, T=10 save
   ioi         ld   (SBCR), a       ; B=3, T=12 disable interrupt
                                    ; B=11, T=35
SP0RxISR_1:
   pop         HL                   ; B=1, T=7 restore registers
   pop         af                   ; B=1, T=7
   ipres                            ; B=2, T=4 restore IPL
   ret                              ; B=1, T=2
                                    ; B=5, T=20
; note: the RTI instruction is not used because the interrupt process
; does not push the interrupt level onto the stack – the Rabbit™ uses
; the IP register instead.

; nbr of instructions = 20          total length = 40 bytes
; total time = 119 / 154 clocks
; the two numbers for the time are due to the jr nz instruction - most
; of the time the branch will be executed.
```

The total time here is not a good parameter to directly compare because the Rabbit™ uses a 2-cycle method to access memory. A more fair comparison would be to divide the clock cycles by two yielding 59, which is still 50% higher than *Sample 1*. Now comparing the two sets of numbers...

The number of instructions shows a 2:1 ratio. This is because the x86/Z180 processors do not have an **O**rthogonal **I**nstruction **S**et. It takes more instructions to perform the same task as compared to a processor that does have an OIS. However, you will notice that the example above has quite a few 1 byte instructions and has only one longer than 3 bytes. The average instruction length is 2 bytes. Whereas *Sample 1*, using the OIS, has an average instruction length of 4 bytes.

Another important point I need to make here is that this ISR will not work properly in the Rabbit™ because the serial port receiver and transmitter use the same interrupt vector. However, I did not want to bias the comparison by implementing the code necessary for detecting between a transmit and a receive interrupt.

Note: it is totally coincidental that Samples 1 and 2 are the same length. I was completely surprised!

Sample 3 uses a technique which will work with any processor that has dedicated registers for each Interrupt Priority Level. Note that the only difference between this one and the previous sample is that this one does not save and restore the registers.

```
SP0RxISR:      ; serial port 0 Rx Interrupt Service Routine

; get the address to store the byte
   copy.4      SP0RxBufferAddr, r0 ; B=6, T=5 get the buffer pointer

; clear the interrupt, read and store the byte
   iocopy.1    SP0DATA, (r0)       ; B=4, T=4 read and store the byte
                                   ; - also clears the interrupt

; update the buffer pointer
   incp.1      r0                  ; B=2, T=2 point to next byte
                                   ; location
   copy.4      r0, SP0RxBufferAddr ; B=6, T=5 save it

; the following instruction could replace the previous two except that
; it takes 1 more clock even though it is 2 less bytes. Incrementing a
; register is much faster than incrementing a pointer in memory.
;  incp.1      SP0RxBufferAddr     ; B=6, T=8

; update the byte count - a 2 byte value
   dec.2       SP0RxByteCount      ; B=6, T=6
                                   ; T=22 to this point
; disable the interrupt if done
   bne         SP0RxISRexit        ; B=2, T=3/2 branch if not done
                                   ; receiving all bytes
   and.1       #~RXIPL_MASK, SP0INT   ; B=8, T=7 disable the interrupt
```

```
; restore the registers and exit the ISR
SP0RxISRexit:
    reti                              ; B=2, T=6 return from the
                                      ; interrupt

; nbr of instructions = 8            total length = 36 bytes
; total time = 31/37 clocks

; the two numbers for the time are due to the bne instruction - most
; of the time the branch will be executed.
```

There is not a whole lot of difference between Samples 1 and 3 because only one register needed to be saved and restored. If all four were used, an additional 18 clocks would be required for Sample 1. If this processor did not have **pushr** and **popr** instructions even more clocks, as well as bytes, would be required to save and restore the registers.

Sample 4 uses a technique that will only work with a processor that has dedicated registers for each Interrupt Priority Level *and* the program is set up to allow only this one device to execute with the specific IPL. For this ISR to operate correctly the following registers need to be pre-loaded with the appropriate values:

IPL:R0 = address of the buffer to store the bytes
IPL:R1 = count of bytes remaining (2 byte value)
IPL:R2 = address of SP0INT
IPL:R3 = address of SP0DATA

Note that this variation of the ISR is significantly shorter – and faster – than the other two.

```
SP0RxISR:        ; serial port 0 Rx Interrupt Service Routine

; clear the interrupt, read and store the byte
    copy.l      (r3),(r0)             ; B=2, T=3 also clears the
                                      ; interrupt

; update the buffer pointer
    incp.l      r0                    ; B=2, T=2 point to the address to
                                      ; put the next byte

; update the byte count – a 2 byte value
    dbne        r1, SP0RxISRexit      ; B=4, T=3/2 update byte count &
                                      ; branch if not done receiving all
                                      ; bytes

; disable the interrupt if done
```

```
   and.l       #~RXIPL_MASK, (r2)  ; B=4, T=5 clear the interrupt bits

; exit the ISR
SP0RxISRexit:
   reti                            ; B=2, T=6 return from the
                                   ; interrupt

; nbr of instructions = 5total length = 14 bytes
; total time = 14/18 clocks
; The total time obviously does not include the interrupt latency.

; The two numbers for the time are due to the dbne instruction - most
; of the time the branch will be executed, skipping the and
; instruction.
```

One of the reasons for showing three slightly different versions of the ISR is to show that the same problem can have more than one correct solution.
The "best" solution for any given requirement is going to be dependent on several factors. Among them are:

- Development time – how much time do you have to develop a solution? Even while writing these ISRs I went through several solutions that would have worked but I wanted to optimize the code. I had plenty of time to spend. You may not be so fortunate. You may have to go with the first solution that works.

- Speed – you may need to find the solution that executes as fast as possible. This will usually require more development time.

- Instruction set – this is perhaps the most significant factor. Each processor has its own strengths and weaknesses. You must learn to deal with them since they cannot be changed. There is always more than one way to write a program.

Serial Port Transmit

Now lets do the same thing for a transmit ISR using the Sample 3 method. First, an outline of the process. These are the steps which must be accomplished – not necessarily in this order:

- Clear the interrupt
- Get the byte from the buffer
- Transmit the byte
- Update the byte count and buffer pointer as required
- Restore the registers (not necessary for this processor)
- Return from the interrupt

You might want to try to write the code yourself before looking at this solution!

```
#vector          VECTOR_SP0TX         ; tell the assembler the interrupt
                                      ; vector address
SP0TxISR:        ; serial port 0 Tx Interrupt Service Routine

; get the address of the byte
    copy.4       SP0TxBufferAddr, r0 ; B=6, T=5 get the address of the
                                      ; byte to transmit

; clear the interrupt, read and store the byte
    iocopy.1     (r0), SP0DATA        ; B=4, T=4 read and transmit the
                                      ; byte - also clears the interrupt

; update the buffer pointer
    incp.1       SP0TxBufferAddr      ; B=6, T=8

; update the byte count - a 2 byte value
    dec.2        SP0TxByteCount       ; B=6, T=6

; disable the interrupt if done
    bne          SP0TxISRexit         ; B=2, T=3/2 branch if not done
                                      ; receiving all bytes
    ioand.1      #~TXIPL_MASK, SP0INT   ; B=6, T=6 disable the
                                        ; interrupt

; exit the ISR
SP0TxISRexit:
    reti                              ; B=2, T=6 return from the
                                      ; interrupt

; total length = 32 bytes             total time = 32 / 37 clocks
; the two numbers for the time are due to the bne instruction - most
; of the time the branch will be executed, skipping the ioand
; instruction.
```

Comparing this to Sample 3 above you will see that they are almost identical.

12 Exercises

Exercise 5

Let's start off with a purely mathematical function that solves a common equation – a polynomial expression of the form: $Y = a + bX + cX^2 + dX^3 + ...$ Except we will do it for the general case where the order of the polynomial is a parameter. The easiest way to set this up is to define the criteria for calling a function which will perform the calculations. The only rule we need is to state that each of the required values are in a structure defined as follows using C notation:

```
struct Polynomial {
   int     Order;                // order of the polynomial is the
                                 // highest exponent value
   float   X;                    // the value of X
   float   Multiplier[MaxOrder+1];     // array of multipliers -
                                       // with the lowest order
                                       // multiplier first

}
```

Note that a 3rd order equation will have three multipliers and a constant so the array will contain one value more than the number which is the order of the equation. The constant can also be considered as the multiplier for the X^0 value – any value to the 0 power is 1.

This function will be written without doing all of the memory setup that would normally be required if this was to be a complete program. The only requirement is that the address of the structure is passed to the function in R0. This is a common method used in many systems – the first parameter is usually passed in one of the general purpose registers as well as on the stack. It is also common to pass the result back to the caller in one of the general registers.

The function should start with a comment block describing what the function does, all input requirements, what registers and memory locations are used and how the results will be returned to the caller. It could also contain an outline, in pseudo-code, of the function.

```
/* Polynomial - this function will calculate the value of Y given all
the parameters for a polynomial.
Enter with:  0 = address of the structure
             the structure must be stored as follows:
             #alloc.2    integer: order of the polynomial
             #alloc.4    SPFP: the value of X
             #alloc.4    SPFP: array of multipliers - lowest order
                         first
Exit with:   R0 = Y
Register usage:          R0, R1, R2, R3

Here is an outline of the algorithm:

   get the Order of the polynomial and the value of X from the
   structure
   initialize the Multiplicand to x^0 = 1
   initialize Result to 0
   initialize a pointer to the array of multipliers
   Loop:
      Result = Result + Multiplicand * (pointer to array)
      Multiplicand = Multiplicand * X
      increment pointer to point to next Multiplier value in array
      decrement Order and branch to Loop if positive
                                 (note: 0 is positive)
   Result now has the answer.

This algorithm makes use of a feature which is not available in most
processors: using two halves of a register as independent registers.
This can be done because the instructions only operate on the number
of bytes defined by the <size> value specified in the instruction.
Some processors have alternate register sets which can be used such as
are available in the X86 processors and derivatives. Other processors
may have enough registers to handle the algorithm without resorting to
other "tricks".

As stated earlier in this book, one of the keys to efficient assembly
language programming for any processor is a really good understanding
of its register set.
*/
Polynomial:
; get the Order of the polynomial and the value of X from the
; structure
   copy.4      R0, R3             ; copy address of structure
   copy.2      (R3), R1           ; get the order of the polynomial
```

```
   swap.4      R1                ; use "other" 4 bytes for multiplicand
   fpis        #1                ; initialize the multiplicand to 1.0
   copy.4      R0, R1            ; copy for algorithm
   swap.4      R1                ; get order of the polynomial into low
                                 ; bytes
   incp.2      R3                ; point to the X value
   copy.4      (R3), R2          ; get the X value
   incp.4      R3                ; point to the array of multipliers
   swap.4      R3                ; use "other" 4 bytes for answer
   clr.4       R3                ; initialize the answer
   swap.4      R3                ; retrieve array address

; R0 = floating point accumulator
; R1 = order of the polynomial and multiplicand
; R2 = X
; R3 = address of the X0 multiplier and answer

Polynomial_1:
; Result = Result + Multiplicand * (pointer to array)
   swap.4      R1                ; retrieve multiplicand
   copy.4      R1, R0            ; get working copy of multiplicand
   fpsmul      (R3)              ; R0 = multiplier * multiplicand
   swap.4      R3                ; get Result into low 4 bytes
   fpsadd      R3                ; R0 = Result + multiplier *
                                 ; multiplicand

; the following instructions are setting up for the next iteration of
; the loop
   copy.4      R0, R3            ; save it
   swap.4      R3                ; retrieve address of Multiplier array

; Multiplicand = Multiplicand * X
   copy.4      R1, R0            ; get multiplicand
   fpsmul      R2                ; R0 = multiplicand * X
   copy.4      R0, R1            ; save it

; increment pointer to point to next Multiplier value in array
   incp.4      R3                ; update pointer to array

; decrement Order and branch to Loop if not 0
   swap.4      R1                ; retrieve order of the polynomial
   dbge        R1, Polynomial_1  ; branch if not done

; Result now has the answer
```

```
swap.4     R3                  ; retrieve answer
copy.4     R3, R0              ; save for return to caller
rets
```

Here is a spreadsheet detailing all of the instructions as they get executed for this particular instance of a third order polynomial equation: X = 4.0, a = 5.0, b = 6.0, c = 7.0 and d = 8.0. This expands to:

$$Y = Y = 5 \cdot 4^0 + 6 \cdot 4^1 + 7 \cdot 4^2 + 8 \cdot 4^3 = 5 + 24 + 112 + 512 = 653$$

Equation: Y = 5 + 6X + 7X^2 + 8X^3
Structure:
int: Order of polynomial = 3
float: X = 4.0
float: Multipliers = 5.0, 6.0, 7.0, 8.0

Only the register which is modified by the instruction is shown in the table.
Register notation: upper 4 bytes, lower 4 bytes
Since R3 is used as a pointer, its notation will show the value to which it is pointing in parentheses.

copy.4 R0, R3	R3: Z, (3)	R3 = address of the 3 in the structure
copy.2 (R3), R1	R1: Z, 3	
swap.4 R1	R1: 3, Z	
fpis #1	R0: Z, 1.0	
copy.4 R0, R1	R1: 3, 1.0	
swap.4 R1	R1: 1.0, 3	
incp.2 R3	R3: Z, (4.0)	
copy.4 (R3), R2	R2: Z, 4.0	
incp.4 R3	R3: Z, (5.0)	
swap.4 R3	R3: (5.0), Z	
clr.4 R3	R3: (5.0), 0.0	
swap.4 R3	R3: 0.0, (5.0)	

Fig. 12.1

; R0 = floating point accumulator
; R1 = order of the polynomial and multiplicand
; R2 = X (note that R2 is never modified during execution of the algorithm)
; R3 = address of the X^0 multiplier and answer

The loop will be executed four times. Here are the first two iterations:

Polynomial_1:	R2: Z, 4.0		
swap.4 R1	R1: 3, 1.0	R1: 2, 4.0	retrieve multiplicand
copy.4 R1, R0	R0: Z, 1.0	R0: Z, 4.0	get working copy of multiplicand
fpsmul (R3)	R0: Z, 5.0	R0: Z, 24.0	R0 = multiplier * multiplicand
swap.4 R3	R3: (5.0), 0.0	R3: (6.0), 5.0	get Result into low 4 bytes
fpsadd R3	R0: Z, 5.0	R0: Z, 29.0	R0 = Result + multiplier * multiplicand
copy.4 R0, R3	R3: (5.0), 5.0	R3: (6.0), 29.0	save it
swap.4 R3	R3: 5.0, (5.0)	R3: 29.0, (6.0)	retrieve address of Multiplier array
copy.4 R1, R0	R0: Z, 1.0	R0: Z, 4.0	get multiplicand
fpsmul R2	R0: Z, 4.0	R0: Z, 16.0	R0 = multiplicand * X
copy.4 R0, R1	R1: 3, 4.0	R1: 2, 16.0	save it
incp.4 R3	R3: 5.0, (6.0)	R3: 29.0, (7.0)	update pointer to array
swap.4 R1	R1: 4.0, 3	R1: 16.0, 2	retrieve order of the polynomial
dbge R1, Polynomial_1	R1: 4.0, 2	R1: 16.0, 1	

Fig. 12.2

Here are the last two iterations:			
Polynomial_1:	R2: Z, 4.0		
swap.4 R1	R1: 1, 16.0	R1: 0, 64.0	retrieve multiplicand
copy.4 R1, R0	R0: Z, 16.0	R0: Z, 64.0	get working copy of multiplicand
fpsmul (R3)	R0: Z, 112.0	R0: Z, 512.0	R0 = multiplier * multiplicand
swap.4 R3	R3:(7.0), 29.0	R3: (8.0), 141.0	get Result into low 4 bytes
fpsadd R3	R0: Z, 141.0	R0: Z, 653.0	R0 = Result + multiplier * multiplicand
copy.4 R0, R3	R3: (7.0), 141.0	R3: (8.0), 653.0	save it
swap.4 R3	R3: 141.0, (7.0)	R3: 653.0, (8.0)	retrieve address of Multiplier array
copy.4 R1, R0	R0: Z, 16.0	R0: Z, 64.0	get multiplicand
fpsmul R2	R0: Z, 64.0	R0: Z, 512.0	R0 = multiplicand * X
copy.4 R0, R1	R1: 1, 64.0	R1: 0, 512.0	save it
incp.4 R3	R3: 141.0, (8.0)	R3: 653.0, (??)	update pointer to array
swap.4 R1	R1: 64.0, 1	R1: 512.0, 0	retrieve order of the polynomial
dbge R1, Polynomial_1	R1: 64.0, 0	R1: 512.0, -1	
The final answer is:			
swap.4 R3		R3: (??), 653.0	
copy.4 R3, R0		R0: Z, 653.0	
rets			

Fig. 12.3

The tables contains the one-time code:

If you analyze the register values closely you will note that the second instruction of the loop can be removed and the first instruction can be moved further down to immediately preceding the instruction: *copy.4 R1, R0*. They were in place in order to make the algorithm easier to follow.

Another possible increase in efficiency can be implemented by updating R1 (the order count) immediately after the *fpsadd* instruction and exiting the loop if it is negative. The final instruction in the loop would then be *br Polynomial_1*. The reason this is a "possible" increase in efficiency is that there would be the additional *br* instruction executed for every iteration except the last. there might also have to be some movement of the *swap* instructions and possibly adding some.

Exercise 6

Task: implement two ISRs:

- Real Time clock which maintains the seconds, minutes, hours, and days the program has been running.
- A timer with 1 millisecond resolution.

```
/* First it would be a good idea to outline the entire process:
   1.  The initialization set-up just like the previous exercises and
       samples
   2.  Program code
       (a) Set the startup vector
```

```
        (b) Initialize the Stack Pointer
        (c) Initialize all RAM values as required by the ISRs.
        (d) Enable the interrupts
    3.  RTC ISR
    4.  Timer ISR
*/

;*********************** Memory Definitions ********************

;           define the RAM values
#define     RAMSTART        0x40000         ; starting address of RAM
#define     RAMSIZE         0x40000         ; and its size
#define     RAMEND          RAMSTART + RAMSIZE  ; calculate the end
                                                ; address of the RAM

;           define the stack size and location
#define     STACKSIZE       0x1000          ; size of stack
#define     STACK_TOP       RAMEND - STACKSIZE  ; top of the stack

;           define the values for the Address Pointer
#address    NEXT_ROM        0x400           ; starting address to put any
                                            ; constants
#address    NEXT_PC         0x1000          ; starting address of the
                                            ; program
#address    NEXT_RAM        RAMSTART        ; start of the RAM

;************************************************************
; Define any other constants that may be needed for this task
; *** Other values

;************************************************************
; Interrupt Vectors
; The interrupt vectors will be set using the "alternative" method -
; placing the #vector directive immediately before the code for the
; interrupt itself.

;************************************************************
; Any required constants
#address    NEXT_ROM
;************************************************************
; Any required RAM
#address    NEXT_RAM                        ; set the Address Pointer to
                                            ; the next available RAM
```

```
; allocate the RAM needed to store the time values
Seconds:      #alloc.1
Minutes:      #alloc.1
Hours:        #alloc.1
Days:         #alloc.2
; millisecond time value used by Timer F ISR
MilliSeconds: #alloc.4

#define    BYTES2CLEAR    NEXT_RAM – Seconds    ; calculate the nbr of
                                                ; bytes to clear for
                                                ; initialization

/* Notice the interesting calculation that the assembler can do in
order to calculate the number of bytes used for storing the time
values. NEXT_RAM is a symbol while Seconds is a label; however, you
need to remember that a label is a special case of a symbol.
You should also notice that the assembler seems to allocate two bytes
for Hours. This is because the next #alloc is for two bytes - the as-
sembler automatically aligns it to an even address.

Even though it is not part of this exercise, it would be possible for
this "structure" to maintain real date information if a program is
written to first enter the current date and time into it. The
structure could easily be expanded to include the month and year. The
additional values would be: DayOfMonth, Month and Year. In order to do
this properly, there would also be a table of constants containing the
number of days for each month. A special test or a separate table
would be required to handle Leap Year.
*/

;************************************************************
; Program code

#if NEXT_ROM >= NEXT_PC
   #error "NEXT_ROM incursion into NEXT_PC"
#endif

#address   NEXT_PC                       ; set the Address Pointer to
                                         ; the start of the program
#vector    VECTOR_START                  ; set up the start up vector
                                         ; to point to the first
                                         ; instruction
```

```
;************** begin initialization code **************************
; first set up the stack pointer
   copy.4     #RAMTOP, SP        ; set up the stack pointer to the top
                                 ; of the RAM
   setipl     0                  ; enable interrupts

; initialize RAM values
   copy.2     #BYTES2CLEAR, r0   ; get number of bytes in the Time
                                 ; structure
   copy.4     #Seconds, r1       ; get the address to start clearing
Main_1:
   clr.1      (r1)               ; clear a byte
   incp.1     r1                 ; point to the next byte
   dbne       r0, Main_1         ; update byte count and branch if not
                                 ; done all bytes

/* The above is a general purpose routine which will clear any number
of contiguous bytes. Knowing that there are only nine bytes to be
cleared a much shorter set of instructions is:
   clr.1      Seconds            ; clear the first byte
   clr.8      Seconds+1          ; clear the remaining bytes
This is the appropriate point to insert code to enable the RTC
interrupt
*/

/* set up a 1 millisecond interrupt using Timer F
When programming an I/O device, it is a good idea to have a
description of all the registers handy. Review each register to see
what needs to be programmed. When writing the code to set up an ISR,
you should enable the interrupt as the last step.
*/

   iocopy.4   CPU_FREQUENCY, r0  ; get the cpu clock frequency – in Hz
   div.4      #1000, r0          ; calculate timer divisor for 1kHz
   iocopy.4   r0, TFDATA         ; set timer F divisor
   clr.1      TFCLK              ; use CPU clock
   iocopy.1   #0xC0, TFCFG       ; enable timer F to count using value
                                 ; in TFDATA
   iocopy.1   #1, TFINT          ; enable Timer F interrupt at IPL = 1

Main_end:
   br         Main_end           ; loop forever – since there is no
                                 ; main program for this exercise.
```

```
;******************** RTC_ISR ********************************
#vector       VECTOR_RTC
RTC_ISR:      ; not strictly needed but good for documentation
/* This ISR updates the variables:
   Seconds - byte
   Minutes - byte
   Hours - byte
   Days - word
based on the interrupt occurring once per second.
*/
; the interrupt is cleared simply by servicing it
; update Seconds
   copy.4  #Seconds, r0         ; 3 get the address of the time
                                ; structure
   inc.1   (r0)                 ; 3 update seconds
   comp.1  #60, (r0)            ; 3 done this minute?
   bgt     RTC_ISR_EXIT         ; 3/2 br if no
   clr.1   (r0)                 ; 2 start new minute – seconds = 0
; update Minutes
   incp.1  r0                   ; 2 point to Minutes
   inc.1   (r0)                 ; 3 update
   comp.1  #60, (r0)            ; 3 done this hour?
   bgt     RTC_ISR_EXIT         ; 3/2 br if no
   clr.1   (r0)                 ; 2 start new hour – minutes = 0
; update Hours
   incp.1  r0                   ; 2 point to Hours
   inc.1   (r0)                 ; 3 update
   comp.1  #24, (r0)            ; 3 done this day?
   bgt     RTC_ISR_EXIT         ; 3/2 br if no
   clr.1   (r0)                 ; 3 start new day – hours = 0
; update Days
   incp.1  r0                   ; 2 point to Days
   inc.2   (r0)                 ; 3 update
RTC_ISR_EXIT:
   reti                         ; 6

/* Most of the interrupts will just update the Seconds count which
takes a total of 18 clocks plus the interrupt latency. If all values
need to be updated, the total is 49 clocks plus the interrupt latency.

Assuming an average instruction takes 4 clocks, the latency will be 12
clocks:
   4 for the current instruction to finish
   3 to push the PC onto the stack
```

```
   2 to push the PSR onto the stack
   2 to retrieve the address of the ISR from the vector table
   1 to place the ISR address into the PC
This will yield between 30 and 61 clocks total to service the
interrupts.
*/

;********************* Timer F_ISR ****************************
#vector     VECTOR_TMRF     ; use Timer F for the 1 millisecond interrupt
TimerF_ISR:                 ; not strictly needed but good for
                            ; documentation
// This ISR updates the variable MilliSeconds ( 4 bytes )

   iocopy.l    TFSTAT, r0          ; get status and clear the interrupt
   inc.4       MilliSeconds        ; update milliseconds count
   reti
```

Exercise 7

```
/* Exercise_7.asm

Task: Transmit a message from Serial Port 0 and receive a response
terminated with a carriage return. Use the receive (Sample 3) and
transmit ISRs from the ISR chapter.
First it would be a good idea to outline the entire process:
   1. Define the memory configuration values
   2. Define any other constants that may be needed for this task
         (a) Serial port values
         (b) Other values
   3. Interrupt Vectors
   4. Any required constants
   5. Any required RAM
         (a) Pointers
         (b) Buffers
         (c) Counters
   6. Program code
         (a) Set the startup vector
         (b) Initialize the Stack Pointer
         (c) Set up the serial port registers
         (d) Transmit a request message
             i. Write a separate function for transmitting a message
         (e) Get the response
             i. Write a separate function for receiving a response
         (f) Wait forever
```

```
The outline statements above will be inserted into the program code
below as comments. The highest level outline sections will be
indicated with a full line of asterisks. The additional descriptions
for the initialization statements will not be repeated here.
*/

#nprint        PR_PROC_DEFS        ; do not print the standard processor
                                   ; definitions

;********************* Memory Definitions ***********************

;           define the RAM values
#define     RAMSTART        0x40000        ; starting address of RAM
#define     RAMSIZE         0x40000        ; and its size
#define     RAMEND          RAMSTART+ RAMSIZE   ; calculate the end
                                                ; address of the RAM

;           define the stack size and location
#define     STACKSIZE       0x1000         ; size of stack
#define     STACK_TOP       RAMEND - STACKSIZE  ; top of the stack

;           define the values for the Address Pointer
#address    NEXT_ROM        0x400          ; starting address to put any
                                           ; constants
#address    NEXT_PC         0x1000         ; starting address of the
                                           ; program
#address    NEXT_RAM        RAMSTART       ; start of the RAM

;************************************************************
; Define any other constants that may be needed for this task
; *** Serial port values
#define     RXIPL_MASK      0x07           ; mask for the receive IPL
#define     RX0_IPL         0x01           ; IPL for SP0 Rx = 1
#define     TXIPL_MASK      0x70           ; mask for the transmit IPL
#define     TX0_IPL         0x10           ; IPL for SP0 Tx = 1
#define     TX_BUSY         0x80           ; transmitter busy bit
#define     SP0_BAUD        19200          ; baud rate for SP0
#define     SP0RXBUF_SIZE 100              ; define the number of bytes
                                           ; for the serial port Rx
                                           ; buffer
#define     ASCII_CR        0x0D           ; ASCII CR value

;************************************************************
; Any required constants
```

```
#address    NEXT_ROM
Message_1: #alloc.s       "Enter a numeric integer string terminated
                           with"
           #alloc.s       " a carriage return\n\r\0"

;************************************************************
; Any required RAM

#address    NEXT_RAM                       ; set the Address Pointer to
                                           ; the next available RAM

;           pointers, buffers and counters

;           set up the RAM required for Serial Port 0

BaudConstant: #alloc.4                     ; CPU_FREQUENCY/16 needed for
                                           ; calculating USART divisor

SP0RxBuffer:  #allocb.1   SP0RXBUF_SIZE ; allocate the serial port 0
                                           ; Rx buffer
SP0RxByteCount:   #alloc.2                 ; serial port 0 Rx byte count
SP0RxBufferAddr: #alloc.4                  ; serial port 0 Rx buffer
                                           ; pointer

SP0TxByteCount:   #alloc.2                 ; serial port 0 Tx byte count
SP0TxBufferAddr: #alloc.4                  ; serial port 0 Tx buffer
                                           ; pointer

;************************************************************
; Program code

#address    NEXT_PC          ; set the Address Pointer to the start of
                             ; the program
#vector     VECTOR_RTC       ; dummy ISR required by the assembler
 reti
#vector     VECTOR_START     ; set up the start up vector to point to the
                             ; first instruction
;******************** begin initialization code ********************
; first set up the stack pointer
   copy.4     #RAMEND, SP         ; set up the stack pointer to the top
                                  ; of the RAM

; calculate the base frequency value needed by the UARTs
   iocopy.4   CPU_FREQUENCY, r0 ; get the cpu frequency
```

```
   div.4      #16, r0            ; base divisor for the USART baud rate
                                 ; calculations
   copy.4     r0, BaudConstant   ; save for other USARTs if necessary

; set up Parallel Port 0.0 for Serial Port 0 Tx and Parallel Port 0.1
; as input.
   iocopy.1   #4, PP0.0CFG       ; PP0.0 = SP0 Tx
   clr.1      PP0.1CFG           ; PP0.1 = input

; Set up the serial port registers. Since it is possible for the
; program to restart without a reset, it is usually a good idea to set
; up all the registers.

   div.4      #SP0_BAUD, r0      ; calculate baud divisor for SP0
   iocopy.2   r0, SP0DIV         ; set the baud rate
   iocopy.1   #1, SP0RPORT       ; SP0 Rx to use PP0.1
   iocopy.1   #0x10, SP0CFG      ; Asynchronous, 1 stop bit, no parity,
                                 ; 8 data bits
   clr.1      SP0CLK             ; use internal clock
   clr.1      SP0INT             ; disable serial port interrupts
   setipl     0                  ; enable interrupts
;********************* end initialization code *********************

; now send a message and receive a message
   copy.4     #Message_1, r0     ; the transmit function requires the
                                 ; message address in r0
   callr      Send_Message_w     ; transmit the message and wait for it
                                 ; to complete
   copy.4     #SP0RxBuffer, r0   ; the receive function requires the
                                 ; buffer address in r0
   callr      Rcv_Message_w      ; receive a message and wait for the
                                 ; carriage return
Loop:
   br         Loop               ; wait forever

;**************** Receive and Transmit Functions *****************

/* A few comments about the following functions (which should be true
about all functions):
  - comments at the beginning describe:
      what is necessary for calling the function
      what the function has to do for the ISR - if applicable
      how the function exits
      all status return values - if applicable
```

```
      a description of all register and RAM usage
   - each statement has a meaningful comment based on context
   - a comment describing each block of statements
   - the format of the internal labels insures no duplication
   - the function name at the end allows you to know what function it
     is
   - when scrolling from below
   - the comments line up (as much as is practical) making it easy to
     read
*/

/********************** Send_Message_w ***********************
Send_Message_w - transmit a message via serial port 0 and wait for the
message to complete.

Enter with:
   R0 = the address of the message terminated with a 0 - the 0 byte
   will not be transmitted.

Uses:         R0, R1, R2
Initializes: SP0TxBufferAddr and SP0TxByteCount (the ISR updates
             these values)
Enables:      SP0 Tx interrupt and sends the first byte of the message.
             The remaining bytes are sent by the ISR

The ISR expects:
   SP0TxBufferAddr = address of the message to be sent
   SP0TxByteCount = the number of bytes to be transmitted
   the interrupt to be enabled
   the first byte to be sent
The ISR will disable the interrupt when done

Note: since this is not an ISR, the number of clocks is not indicated.
*/

Send_Message_w:

; count the number of bytes in the message
   copy.4     r0, r1              ; get a working copy of the message
                                  ; address
   clr.2      r2                  ; initialize the byte count
Send_Message_w_1:
   test.1     (r1)                ; end of message?
   beq        Send_Message_w_2    ; br if yes
```

```
   inc.2       r2                  ; update byte count
   incp.1      r1                  ; update pointer to the message
   br          Send_Message_w_1    ; loop until done

Send_Message_w_2:
; adjust for the first byte and set up the values required by the ISR
   copy.1      (r0), r1            ; get first byte to be transmitted
   dec.2       r2                  ; adjust for
   incp.1      r0                  ; first byte
   copy.2      r2, SP0TxByteCount    ; copy the byte count for the ISR
   copy.4      r0, SP0TxBufferAddr   ; point to the message to be sent

; enable interrupt and send the first byte - must be done in this
; order. If not, the interrupt will be missed. Since the Tx Shift
; Register is empty the byte will be transferred immediately from the
; Data register to the TSR.

   ioor.1      #TX0_IPL, SP0INT    ; set Tx IPL - assume it was
                                   ; previously disabled
   iocopy.1    r1, SP0DATA         ; send the first byte

; wait for the transmitter to get done
Send_Message_w_3:
   test.2      SP0TxByteCount      ; have all bytes have been
                                   ; transmitted?
   bne         Send_Message_w_3    ; br if no
Send_Message_w_4:
   iotst.1     #TX_BUSY, SP0STAT   ; has last byte has completed?
   bcs         Send_Message_w_4    ; br if no
   rets
; Send_Message_w

/*********************** Rcv_Message_w ***********************

Rcv_Message_w - receive a message via serial port 0 and wait for a
carriage return

Enter with:
   R0 = the address to put the message
Return with:
   success:            R0 = address of terminating null
   buffer overflow:    R0 = 0
Note: This function could simply use the value of SP0RxByteCount (= 0)
to indicate overflow but that places the burden on the caller to know
```

```
ISR details. The purpose of this "driver" is to isolate the main
program from having to know those details.

Uses:           R0
Initializes:    SP0RxBufferAddr and SP0RxByteCount (the ISR updates
                these values)
Enables:        SP0 Rx interrupt and then disables it upon receiving
                a CR

The ISR expects:
   SP0RxBufferAddr    = address of the message to be sent
   SP0RxByteCount     = the number of bytes to be received
   the interrupt to be enabled

The ISR will disable the interrupt if the byte count reaches 0. Since
this function is looking for a specific character it loads the byte
count value with a larger number than what is expected and this
function will disable the interrupt.

Note: since this is not an ISR, the number of clocks is not indicated.
*/

Rcv_Message_w:
; set up values for ISR
   copy.4     r0, SP0RxBufferAddr     ; tell ISR where to put the
                                      ; characters
   copy.2     #SP0RXBUF_SIZE-1, SP0RxByteCount     ; set byte count to
                                                   ; buffer size
   ioor.1     #RX0_IPL, SP0INT   ; set Rx IPL - assumes it was
                                 ; previously disabled

; wait for a CR character: r0 still points to the buffer starting
; address
Rcv_Message_w_1:
   test.2     SP0RxByteCount     ; is buffer full?
   beq        Rcv_Message_w_2    ; br if yes - overflow!
   comp.4     r0, SP0RxBufferAddr    ; has buffer address changed?
   bne        Rcv_Message_w_1    ; br if no
   comp.1     (r0), #ASCII_CR    ; is the new byte a CR?
   beq        Rcv_Message_w_3    ; br if yes
   incp.1     r0                 ; point to next byte location in
                                 ; buffer
   br         Rcv_Message_w_1    ; wait for next byte
```

```
; handle overflow
Rcv_Message_w_2:
   clr.4      r0                   ; show overflow
   br         Rcv_Message_w_4      ; and exit

; handle the CR
Rcv_Message_w_3:
   clr.1      (r0)                 ; replace CR with null
Rcv_Message_w_4:
   ioand.1    #~RXIPL_MASK, SP0INT    ; disable the Rx interrupt
   rets
; Rcv_Message_w

; the ISRs are duplicated here for completeness
;********************** VECTOR_SP0RX ************************

/* SP0RxBufferAddr must be initialized to the start of the receive
buffer - incremented by the ISR.
SP0RxByteCount must be initialized to the number of bytes to be
received - decremented by the ISR.
The interrupt is disabled if/when this count reaches 0.
The main program must enable SP0 interrupts - this should be done
last.
*/
#vector    VECTOR_SP0RX            ; tell the assembler the interrupt
                                   ; vector address
SP0RxISR:                          ; serial port 0 Rx Interrupt Service
                                   ; Routine

; get the address to store the byte
   copy.4     SP0RxBufferAddr, r0    ; B=6, T=5 get the buffer pointer

; clear the interrupt, read and store the byte
   iocopy.1   SP0DATA, (r0)        ; B=4, T=4 read and store the byte
                                   ; - also clears the interrupt

; update the buffer pointer
   incp.1     r0                   ; B=2, T=2 point to next byte
                                   ; location
   copy.4     r0, SP0RxBufferAddr    ; B=6, T=5 save it

; the following instruction could replace the previous two except
; that: it takes 1 more clock - even though it is 2 bytes less.
; Incrementing a register is much faster than incrementing a pointer
```

```
; in memory.
;  incp.l     SP0RxBufferAddr   ; B=6, T=8

; update the byte count - a 2 byte value
   dec.2      SP0RxByteCount    ; B=6, T=6
                                ; B=24, T=22 to this point
; disable the interrupt if done
   bne        SP0RxISRexit      ; B=2, T=2/3 branch if not done
                                ; receiving all bytes
   ioand.l    #~RXIPL_MASK, SP0INT    ; B=6, T=6  disable the
                                      ; interrupt

; restore the registers and exit the ISR
SP0RxISRexit:
   reti                         ; B=2, T=6 return from the interrupt

; nbr of instructions = 8       total length = 34 bytes
; total time = 36/31 clocks

;*********************** VECTOR_SP0TX ***********************

/*
SP0TxBufferAddr must be initialized to the start of the message to be
sent - incremented by the ISR.

SP0TxByteCount must be initialized to the number of bytes to be
transmitted - decremented by the ISR. The interrupt is disabled when
this count reaches 0.
*/

#vector VECTOR_SP0TX            ; tell the assembler the interrupt
                                ; vector address
SP0TxISR:                       ; serial port 0 Tx Interrupt Service
                                ; Routine

   copy.4     SP0TxBufferAddr, r0   ; B=6, T=5 get the address of the
                                    ; next byte
   iocopy.l   (r0), SP0DATA     ; B=4, T=4 get and transmit the
                                ; byte, also clears the interrupt
   incp.l     r0                ; B=2, T=2 point to next byte
                                ;location
   copy.4     r0, SP0TxBufferAddr   ; B=6, T=5 save it
   dec.2      SP0TxByteCount    ; B=6, T=6 update the byte count
                                ; - a 2 byte value
```

```
                                ; B=24, T=22 to this point
   bne         SPOTxISRexit     ; B=2, T=2/3 branch if not done
                                ; receiving all bytes
   ioand.l     #~TXIPL_MASK, SPOINT   ; B=6, T=6 disable the interrupt

SPOTxISRexit:
   reti                         ; B=2, T=6 return from the interrupt

; nbr of instructions = 8       total length = 34 bytes
; total time = 36/31 clocks

; the two numbers for the time are due to the bne instruction -
; most of the time the branch will be executed.

/* If you are really concerned about ISR time you should also account
for interrupt latency - for this processor it is 8 + nbr of clocks
remaining in the instruction being executed when the interrupt occurs.
A good average for instruction time is about 6 clocks.
*/
```

13 An Alternate Processor Architecture and Instruction Set

In this chapter an alternate processor architecture will be partially developed. The primary goals are to demonstrate that a different processor architecture can have an almost identical instruction set and that it does not have to be a traumatic experience going from one processor to another.

The first instruction set discussed in this book will be referred to as IS 1 while this new one will be IS 2. There is a pre-defined symbol INSTRUCTION_SET that you can evaluate in the program to ensure that the correct instruction set is being used. Its value will be either one or two depending on your selection when you RUN the Assembler.

Here is a summary of the architecture features of the processor which is discussed in this chapter. The following list is almost a copy of the list in Chapter 4. The differences are bolded. Except for these differences, all of the features in Chapters 4 and 5 hold for this processor as well.

- von Neumann memory architecture
- CISC
- Orthogonal Instruction Set
- Little Endian
- 2's-complement binary arithmetic
- Floating point hardware
- Memory Mapped I/O

- 16 bit internal data bus
- 32 bit Program Counter and Stack Pointer
- 16 bit Processor Status Register
- ***Load and Store* architecture**
- **8 sets of fifteen 64 bit general purpose registers + Stack Pointer**
  - The registers may be used as 8, 16, 32 and 64 bits
  - **R15 is the stack pointer**
- 8 interrupt levels, prioritized, each with a dedicated register set
- Dedicated vector addresses in low memory for each interrupt
- Program Counter and Processor Status Register pushed onto stack for interrupts
- When the processor comes out of Reset
  - The IPL is set to 7, effectively disabling interrupts
  - The content of address 0 (4 bytes) is placed into the Program Counter

As you can see, there are not very many differences. The major difference in this architecture is that it is of the *Load and Store* type (see Chapter 7 for some other examples). However, this difference is considerable! In this *Load and Store* processor *all math and logic operations occur in registers*.

For most instructions the destination must be a register – no address modes allowed. The one exception is the COPY instruction which allows an address mode for either argument but not both. This instruction set is closer to a pure *Load and Store* than many processors available today.

IS 1 example:

```
copy.2   SourceLoc, DestLoc   ; copy the contents of address
                              ; SourceLoc to address DestLoc
```

IS 2 example:

```
copy.2   SourceLoc, r0  ; copy the contents of SourceLoc to r0
copy.2   r0, DestLoc    ; copy the contents of r0 to DestLoc
```

The IS 1 instruction takes 10 bytes and 7 clocks. The two replacement instructions for IS 2 take 12 bytes and 8 clocks. Obviously a little bit less efficient. However, if most of the instructions in a given block of code operate on registers with few, if any, memory references, the IS 2 instructions will take the same amount of memory and execute in the same number of clocks. Also, since IS 2 has more registers in each set, it is quite possible that fewer memory references will be required, thereby making it more efficient! Another possible advantage for this architecture is that it might be easier to implement pipelining in the CPU and thus reduce the effective number of clock cycles per instruction.

Just as a general note the address mode timing and sizes are the same for both processors. Also, these descriptions will not be as complete as those in Chapter 8.

Double Operand Integer

The differences between the IS 1 instructions and those for IS 2 are:

> Address modes are not allowed for either the source or the destination – except COPY.
>
> The COPY instruction allows only one of the two arguments to have an address mode.
>
> All instructions (except some COPYs) are 2 bytes.
>
> The Total Execution Time = Instruction Fetch + Operation Clocks. For most instructions the total will be 2 Clocks.

There are two instructions in the IS 1 set that allow access to the Stack Pointer: ADD and COPY. There are no similar restrictions in the IS 2 set. The main difference is that the SP is R15 and can be referenced using either notation. Since the instructions are nearly identical they will not be listed again here but will be demonstrated with a single instruction as well as more details on COPY.

During the writing of this book, I initially used two instructions instead of COPY: LD and ST, for load and store. I even implemented the assembler to handle them. This would have made the architecture more obvious. However, after writing a few samples, I decided that using the COPY would make it easier to write programs that will run using either instruction set. Also, I was having trouble remembering which instruction used a register as the source/destination.

With this implementation all you need to remember is that one of the arguments needs to be a simple register reference.

Keep in mind that for ALL these DOI instructions the source is still the first argument.

ADD: Add the source register, using twos-complement arithmetic, to the destination register.

Operation Clocks: 1

Example:

```
add.2       R8, R12         ; add the 2 byte value in R8 to the
                            ; contents of R12
```

Condition Codes:

N = x: = value of the result MSB: = 1 if result is negative
Z = x: = 1 if result = 0
C = x: Only valid for *unsigned* values:
C = 1 if the result does not fit in the specified data size,
V = x: Only valid for *signed* values:
V = 1 if both values are the same sign but the result is the opposite sign,

Note that is is possible for both the C-bit and the V-bit to be set by the same instruction.

The above description is essentially identical to that for the IS 1 instruction.

COPY: Copy the source operand to the destination. Address modes may be used for only one argument.

Execution Time: 1 + argument + 0

Condition Codes:

N = x: = value of MSB
Z = x: = 1 if value = 0
C = n
V = n

Examples with a register as destination:

```
copy.2  #15, R0         ; copy a 2 byte value of 15 to
                        ; register 0
                        ; K=1,   T=1+K+0=2, B=2+2*K+0=4
copy.1  r1, r2          ; T=1, B=2
copy.2  (r3), r4        ; T=1+1=2, B=2
copy.4  2(r5), r6       ; T=1+1+1+2=5, B=4
copy.8  SourceLoc, r7
```

Examples with a register as source:

```
copy.2  R0, (R10)                ; copy a 2 byte value from R0 to the
                                 ; address in R10
                                 ; K=1, T=1+K+0=2, B=2+0+0=2
copy.2  r2, 10(r3)               ; T=1+1+1+1=4, B=4
copy.4  r4, DestinationLoc       ; T=1+2+2=5, B=6
```

Single Operand Integer

All these instructions must have a register as the argument, otherwise they are identical to those of IS 1.

Floating Point

Since these instructions already have a default destination of R0 there are no changes except that the argument must be a register. Note that the COPY instruction can be used to load a register with an immediate floating point value.

Register Set

These instructions are identical to those of IS 1 except for rexch and rcopy:

In IS 1 you can exchange a single register

In IS 2 you can exchange as many as you want

Examples

```
rexch   0b1001, 7      ; exchange R0 & R3 to RS7
rcopy   0b0110, 3      ; exchange R1 & R2 to RS3
```

These two instructions are four bytes each

Program Counter

These instructions are identical to those of IS 1.

Short I/O

These instructions are identical to those of IS 1. To be completely a “Load and Store” processor would require that these instructions be made to use only registers as the “other” argument. However, most processors will “violate” some rules in order to make programming more efficient.

Block Copy

These instructions are identical to those of IS 1.

Status Register and Miscellaneous

These instructions are identical to those of IS 1 except for PSRCOPY must use a register as a destination.

Examples

Here is the code from an IS 1 example:

```
    copy.4    #PP2.4CFG, r0   ; r0 = address of the I/O register
Main_6:                       ; need a label for the loop
    copy.1    #2|BIT03, (r0) ; 3 bit 4 = 1
    copy.1    #2, (r0)        ; 3 bit 4 = 0
    br        Main_6          ; 3
                              ; total loop time = 9 clocks: duty
                              ; cycle = 3/9 = 33%
```

If it is modified to use only registers in the loop then the IS 1 and IS 2 instructions are identical.

```
    copy.4    #PP2.4CFG, r0   ; r0 = address of the I/O register
    copy.1    #2|BIT03, r1
    copy.1    #2, r2
Main_6:                       ; need a label for the loop
    copy.1    r1, (r0)        ; 2 bit 4 = 1
    copy.1    r2, (r0)        ; 2 bit 4 = 0
    br        Main_6          ; 3
                              ; total loop time = 7 clocks: duty
                              ; cycle = 2/7 = 29%
```

Now for an example using the ISR from Example 6. The original code from IS 1 is shown as a comment with the code for IS 2 on the following line(s):

```
; update Seconds
;  copy.4    #Seconds, r0     ; 3 get the address of the time
                              ; structure
   copy.4    #Seconds, r0     ; 3

; first some initialization not needed for IS 1
   copy.1    #60, r2          ; 2 used to check seconds and minutes
```

```
    clr.2       r3                  ; 1 used to reset counters

;   inc.l       (r0)                ; 3 update seconds
    copy.l      (r0), rl            ; 2
    inc.l       rl                  ; 2 Rl contains updated seconds
    copy.l      rl, (r0)            ; 2 save it

;   comp.l      #60, (r0)           ; 3 done this minute?
    comp.l      r2, rl              ; 2 done this minute? (r2 = #60)

;   bgt         RTC_ISR_EXIT        ; 3/2 br if no
    bgt         RTC_ISR_EXIT        ; 3/2 br if no

;   clr.l       (r0)                ; 2 start new minute - seconds = 0
    copy.l      r3, (r0)            ; 2 start new minute - seconds
                                    ; = 0 (r3 = 0)

; update Minutes
;   incp.l      r0                  ; 2 point to Minutes
    incp.l      r0                  ; 2

;   inc.l       (r0)                ; 3 update
    copy.l      (r0), rl            ; 2 get minutes
    inc.l       rl                  ; 2 update it
    copy.l      rl, (r0)            ; 2 save it

;   comp.l      #60, (r0)           ; 3 done this hour?
    comp.l      r2, rl              ; 2 done this hour?(r2 still contains
                                    ; #60)

;   bgt         RTC_ISR_EXIT        ; 3/2 br if no
    bgt         RTC_ISR_EXIT        ; 3/2 br if no

;   clr.l       (r0)                ; 2 start new hour - minutes = 0
    copy.l      r3, (r0)            ; 2 start new hour - minutes = 0
                                    ; (r3 = 0)

; update Hours
;   incp.l      r0                  ; 2 point to Hours
    incp.l      r0                  ; 2

;   inc.l       (r0)                ; 3 update
    copy.l      (r0), rl            ; 2
    inc.l       rl                  ; 2
```

```
        copy.l      rl, (r0)            ; 2

;       comp.l      #24, (r0)           ; 3 done this day?
        copy.l      #24, r2             ; 2
        comp.l      r2, rl              ; 2

;       bgt         RTC_ISR_EXIT        ; 3/2 br if no
        bgt         RTC_ISR_EXIT        ; 3/2

;       clr.l       (r0)                ; 3 start new day - hours = 0
        copy.l      r3, (r0)            ; 2 start new day - hours = 0 (r3 = 0)

; update Days
;       incp.l      r0                  ; 2 point to Days
        incp.l      r0                  ; 2

;       inc.2       (r0)                ; 3 update
        copy.2      (r0), rl            ; 2
        inc.2       rl                  ; 2
        copy.2      rl, (r0)            ; 2

RTC_ISR_EXIT:
;       reti                            ; 6
        reti                            ; 6
```

As is fairly obvious, the *Load and Store* instruction set takes quite a few more instructions (66 bytes vs 46) and clock cycles (62 vs 49).

Please keep in mind that there was no attempt to develop a truly RISC architecture with more efficient instructions. However, these two examples serve to at least indicate that a CISC processor that is NOT of the *Load and Store* type can easily generate more efficient code.

The primary reason is that it generally takes fewer instructions to implement most operations. Therefore, fewer bytes as well as clock cycles are required. As shown in the earlier example however, this is not always the case. Just as an interesting note: if there were 8 registers instead of 16, the extra bit could be used to indicate one of two address modes for the operands: register vs register indirect. Implementing this feature would make the example above almost identical for both processors. However, then the instruction set would not be a true Load and Store architecture.

Here is Example 5 from Chapter 12, this time using the new instruction set. With its larger number of registers the algorithm will not have to do all the swap instructions.

```
/* Polynomial - this function will calculate the value of Y given all
the parameters for a polynomial.

Y = A(0) * X^0 + A(1) * X^1 + A(2) * X^2 + A(3) * X^3 + A(4) * X^4...

Enter with: R0 = address of the structure
   the structure must be stored as follows:
      #alloc.2   integer: order of the polynomial
      #alloc.4   SPFP: the value of X
      #alloc.4   SPFP: array of multipliers - lowest order first
Exit with: R0 = Y

Here is an outline of the algorithm:
   get the Order of the polynomial and the value of X from the
   structure
   initialize the Multiplicand to X^0 = 1
   initialize Result to 0
   initialize a pointer to the array of multipliers
   Loop:
      Result = Result + Multiplicand * (pointer to array)
      Multiplicand = Multiplicand * X
      increment pointer to point to next Multiplier value in array
      decrement Order and branch to Loop if positive
         (note: 0 is positive)
   Result now has the answer.

   R0 = enter with address of structure, exit with result
   R1 = X^n
   R2 = X
   R3 = working address of the structure - pointer to multipliers
   R4 = multiplier
   R5 = order of polynomial, counts down to -1
*/

Polynomial:
; get the Order of the polynomial, value of X, and point to table of
; multipliers
   copy.4     R0, R3           ; copy address of structure
   copy.2     (R3), R5         ; get order
   incp.2     R3               ; point to X
   copy.4     (R3), R2         ; get X
   incp.4     R3               ; point to table of multipliers
   clear.4    R6               ; initialize answer
   copy.4     #0f1.0, R1       ; initialize X^n
```

```
;  R1 = X^n
;  R2 = X
;  R3 = pointing to X^0 multiplier
;  R4 = multiplier
;  R5 = order of polynomial, counts down to -1
;  R6 = answer

   copy.4     R1, R0              ; get initial value of X^n
Polynomial_1:
; Result = Result + Multiplier * X^n
   copy.4     (R3), R4            ; get multiplier
   fpsmul     R4                  ; R0 = R0 * R4 = A(n) * X^n
   fpsadd     R6                  ; R0 = R0 + R6 = (A(n) * X^n) +
                                  ; previous result
; set up for next iteration
   copy.4     R0, R6              ; save answer for next time
   incp.4     R3                  ; point to next multiplier
   copy.4     R2, R0              ; copy of X
   fpsmul     R1                  ; R0 = R0 * R1 => X^(n+1) = X * X(n)
   copy.4     R0, R1              ; save it
   dbge       R4, Polynomial_1
;
   copy.4     R6, R0              ; retrieve answer
   rts
```

This routine is a little shorter (by four instructions) compared to Example 5. The reason is simply the number of available registers. Please also keep in mind that Example 6 uses the swap instruction essentially emulating additional registers. Most real-world processors do not have this feature. If it were not for this feature, Example 6 would be longer.

Appendix I
Instruction Set Summary

Double Operand Integer

ADD	OP2 = OP1 + OP2
AND	OP2 = OP1 & OP2
ASHIFT	shift OP2 by the amount in OP1
BITEST	OP1 & OP2, OP2 not modified
COMP	compare OP1 and OP2 (OP1-OP2)
COPY	OP2 = OP1
DIV	OP2 = OP2/OP1
DIVU	OP2 = OP2/OP1, unsigned
MUL	OP2 = OP1 * OP2
MULU	OP2 = OP1 * OP2, unsigned
OR	OP2 = OP1 | OP2
SUB	OP2 = OP2 - OP1
XOR	OP2 = OP1 xor OP2

Single Operand Integer

ADDC	OP = OP + C-Bit
CLR	OP = 0
COM	OP = –OP
DEC	OP = OP–1
DECP	OP = OP – sizeof(data)
INC	OP = OP + 1
INCP	OP = OP + sizeof(data)
INV	OP = ~OP
POP	retrieve a value from the stack into the OP
PUSH	insert the OP onto the stack
SUBC	OP = OP - C-Bit
SWAP	swap specified bytes of the OP
SXT	sign extend the OP
TEST	set/clear condition codes based on OP

Rotate

RL	rotate OP 1 bit left
RLC	rotate OP 1 bit left thru C-bit
RR	rotate OP 1 bit right
RRC	rotate OP 1 bit right thru the C-bit
RLB	rotate OP 1 byte right
RRB	rotate OP 1 byte left

Shift

SLA	arithmetic shift of OP 1 bit left
SLL	logical shift of OP 1 bit left
SLLC	logical shift OP 1 bit left thru C-bit
SRA	arithmetic shift of OP 1 bit right
SRL	logical shift of OP 1 bit right
SRLC	logical shift OP 1 bit right thru C-bit

Single Precision Floating Point (SPFP): dest = R0

FPIS	convert integer OP to SPFP
FPSADD	R0 = R0 + OP
FPSCOMP SPFP	compare OP and R0
FPSDIV	R0 = R0 / OP
FPSDP	convert SPFP OP to DPFP in R0
FPSMUL	R0 = R0 * OP
FPSI	convert SPFP OP to integer
FPSSUB	R0 = R0 – OP

Double Precision Floating Point (DPFP): dest = R0

FPID	convert integer OP to DPFP
FPDADD	R0 = R0 + OP
FPDCOMP DPFP	compare OP and R0
FPDDIV	R0 = R0 / OP
FPDI	convert DPFP OP to integer
FPDMUL	R0 = R0 * OP
FPDSP	convert DPFP OP to SPFP
FPDSUB	R0 = R0 - OP

Register Set (RS)

POPR	retrieve registers from the stack
PUSHR	insert registers onto the stack

RSCOPY	copy the default RS set to the specified RS
RCOPY	copy one register to the same one in another RS
RSDEF	set default RS
RSEXCH	exchange specified register set with the default RS
REXCH	exchange one register with the same one in another RS

Program Counter

CALL	call subroutine at absolute address
CALLR	call subroutine at relative address
CALLS	call subroutine at short address
JMP	jump to absolute address
JMPR	jump to relative address
JMPS	jump to short address
RETI	return from interrupt
RETS	return from subroutine
WFI	wait for interrupt
DBGE	decrement register and branch if result is >= 0
DBNE	decrement register and branch if result is != 0
BCC	branch if C-bit clear
BCS	branch if C-bit set
BEQ	branch if equal (Z=1)
BGE	branch if greater than or equal
BGT	branch if greater than
BGTU	branch if greater than – unsigned
BLE	branch if less than or equal
BLEU	branch if less than or equal – unsigned
BLT	branch if less than
BMI	branch if minus (N=1)
BNE	branch if not equal (Z=0)
BPL	branch if plus (N=0)
BR	branch – unconditional
BVC	branch if V-bit clear
BVS	branch if V-bit set

Short I/O

IOAND	logical-and source with I/O register
IOCOPY	copy to/from internal I/O
IOOR	logical-or source with I/O register
IOTST	test a specific bit in an I/O register

Block Copy, PSR and Miscellaneous

BC	copy a block of memory or I/O
BCID	block copy, increment destination addr
BCIS	block copy, increment source addr
CCC	clear condition code bit
CCS	set condition code bit
PSRCOPY	copy PSR
SETIPL	set processor Interrupt Priority Level
NOP	no operation

Appendix II
I/O Register Summary

Parallel Port Registers

PPxDATA – (1 byte, R/W, ?) Parallel Port **x** Data Register

PPxCFG – (1 byte, R/W, 0) Parallel Port **x** Default Configuration Register.

Bit(s)	7	6	5, 4	3	2, 1, 0
Input	*Load Value* 0 = 100 K 1= 20 K	0	*Load* 00 = pulldown 01 = pullup 10 = keeper 11 = none	0	*Function* 000 = Input 001 = PPxDATA 010 = use bit 3 for state
Output	*Slew Rate* 0 = Slow 1 = Fast	*Output Type* 0 = CMOS 1 = Open Drain	*Current* 00 = 4 mA 01 = 8 mA 10 = 12 mA 11 = 16 mA	0	

PPx.yCFG – (1 byte, R/W, 0) Parallel Port **x** Bit **y** Configuration Register.

Bit(s)	7	6	5, 4	3	2, 1, 0
Input	*Load Value* 0 = 100 K 1= 20 K	0	*Load* 00 = pulldown 01 = pullup 10 = keeper 11 = none	0	*Function* 000 = Input 001 = PPxDATA 010 = use bit 3 for state 011-111= output function
Output	*Slew Rate* 0 = Slow 1 = Fast	*Output Type* 0 = CMOS 1 = Open Drain	*Current* 00 = 4 mA 01 = 8 mA 10 = 12 mA 11 = 16 mA	*State* 0/1 (only if function = 010)	

Pulse Modulator Registers

PMxCFG – (1 byte, R/W, 0) Pulse Modulator **x** Configuration Register

Bit(s)	7	6, 5, 4	3	2, 1, 0
	Mode 0 = PPM 1 = PWM	Timer nbr	*Edge* 0 = Start 1 = End	IPL

PMxWIDTH – (4 bytes, R/W, 0) Pulse Modulator **x** Width Register

PMxDELAY – (4 bytes, R/W, 0) Pulse Modulator **x** Delay Register

Serial Port Registers

SPxDATA – (2 bytes, R/W, ?) Serial Port **x** Data Register

SPxDIV – (2 bytes, R/W, 0) Serial Port **x** Divisor Register

SPxRPORT – (1 byte, R/W, 0) Serial Port **x** Receive Port

Bit(s)	7	6, 5, 4	3	2, 1, 0
	1 = Start Rx	Parallel Port	0	Bit nbr

SPxCFG – (1 byte, R/W, 0x10) Serial Port **x** Configuration Register

Bit(s)	7	6	5, 4	3, 2, 1, 0
Asynch	0	*Stop Bits* 0 = 1 1 = 2	*Data Bits* 00 = 7 01 = 8 10 = 9 11 = nu	*Parity* 0000 = none 0100 = even 0101 = odd 0110 = space 0111 = mark
Synch (SPI)	1	0 = Master 1 = Slave	*Clock Mode* see Table	number of bits

SPxCLK – (1 byte, R/W, 0) Serial Port **x** Clock Source

Bit(s)	7	6, 5, 4	3	2, 1, 0
	Clock 0 = Int 1 = Ext	Parallel Port	0	Bit nbr

SPxINT – (1 byte, R/W, 0) Serial Port **x** Interrupt Register

Bit(s)	7	6, 5, 4	3	2, 1, 0
	TxBusy	TxIPL	0	RxIPL

SPxSTAT – (1 byte, R, 0) Serial Port **x** Status Register

Bit	7	6	5	4	3	2	1	0
	1 = TxBusy	1 = TxBuf Empty	0	0	1 = RxDone	1 = RxParity	1 = Rx Overrun	0

Timer/Counter Registers

TxDATA – (4 bytes, R/W, 0) Timer **x** Data Register

TxCLK – (1 byte, R/W, 0) Timer **x** Clock Source

Bit(s)	7	6, 5, 4	3, 2, 1, 0
		000 = CPU	PM X
Internal Clock	0	001 = PM X	or
		010 = Tmr X	Tmr X
External Clock	1	Parallel Port	Bit nbr

TxCFG – (1 byte, R/W, 0) Timer **x** Configure Register

Bit(s)	7	6	5, 4	3	2, 1, 0
	State		*Mode*		
	0 = Disabled	0 = Full Count	00 = Free Run	1 = Clear Counter	Clock Prescale
	1 = Enabled	1 = Use Divisor	01 = Use TxStart & TxStop		
			10 = Stop on Overflow		
			11 = Enable while Timer y running		

TxSTART – (1 byte, R/W, 0) Timer **x** Start Select Register

Bit(s)	7	6, 5, 4	3	2, 1, 0
	+ Edge	Parallel Port	– Edge	Bit nbr

TxSTOP – (1 byte, R/W, 0) Timer **x** Stop Select Register

Bit(s)	7	6, 5, 4	3	2, 1, 0
	+ Edge	Parallel Port	– Edge	Bit nbr

Timer y

TxINT – (1 byte, R/W, 0) Timer **x** Interrupt Register

Bit(s)	7	6	5	4	3	2, 1, 0
	Overflow	Start	Stop			IPL

TxSTAT – (1 byte, R, 0) Timer x Status Register

Bit(s)	7	6	5	4	3	2, 1, 0
	Overflow	Start	Stop		Running	

Appendix III Assembler Error and Warning Messages

ERR_END_OF_FILE	premature end of file
ERR_ERROR	message generated by the #error directive
ERR_INV_ADDR_MODE	invalid address mode
ERR_INV_ADDRESS	invalid address
ERR_INV_ARG	invalid argument
ERR_INV_EXPRESSION	invalid expression
ERR_INV_INSTR	invalid instruction
ERR_INV_NEXT_ADDR	invalid NEXT_xxx address
ERR_INV_NEXT_PC	invalid NEX_PC value
ERR_INV_OPERATOR	invalid operator
ERR_INV_VECTOR	invalid vector
ERR_NEXT_PC_ROM_OVERLAP_NEXT_ROM	incursion into NEXT_PC
ERR_NO_RTC_VECTOR	no VECTOR_RTC defined
ERR_NO_START_VECTOR	no VECTOR_START defined
ERR_NOT_A_SYMBOL	"symbol" has an invalid character
ERR_OPENING_FILE	cannot open specified file
ERR_TOO_MANY_INCLUDES	#includes limited to 10
ERR_TOO_MANY_NESTED_IF	#if limited to depth of 10
ERR_UNDEFINED_SYMBOL	attempted use of undefined symbol
WARN_DUP_SYMBOL	duplicate symbol
WARN_INV_ALIGN	invalid alignment, must be one of: 1, 2, 4, 8 or 16 – forced to 2
WARN_INV_ARG	invalid argument
WARN_INV_DATA_SIZE	invalid data size – forced to 2
WARN_INV_OFFSET	invalid offset – forced to 0
WARN_INV_PRINT_PAR	invalid #print value – print flag not modified
WARN_INV_RADIX	invalid radix – radix value not modified
WARN_INV_REG	invalid register – forced to 0
WARN_INV_REGSET	invalid register set – forced to 0

WARN_NOT_A_LABEL	not a label – ignored
WARN_NOT_REG	argument is not a register – forced to 0
WARN_STRING_TOO_LONG	string too long – truncated to max allowed
WARN_SYMBOL_TOO_LONG	symbol name too long – truncated to max allowed
WARN_TOO_MANY_IFDEF	too many ifdef/ifndef – condition forced to false
WARN_TOO_MANY_SYMBOLS	too many symbols – ignored
WARN_WARNING	message generated by the #warn directive

Appendix IV
Opcodes for Instruction Set 1

The notation used below references each group of four bits within the 16 bit instruction.

Instruction summary showing opcode ranges:

Double Operand Integer	– 0–3	.x	.y	.z
Single Operand Integer	– 4-7	.8	.y	.z
Rotate and Shift	– 4-7	.9	.y	.z
Floating Point	– 4-7	.A	.y	.z
Register Set	– 4-7	.B	.y	.z
Short I/O	– 4-7	.C	.0-4	.z
Block Copy	– 4-7	.C	.8	.0-2
Condition Code	– 4	.C	.8	.8-F
Jump/Call	– 4	.D	.y	.z
Decrement and Branch	– 8-9	.x	.yz	
Branch	– A	.x	.yz	
NOP	– F	.F	.F	.F

Notation used in most instructions:

nn = size of operand (number of bytes): 0=1 byte, 1=2 bytes, 2=4 bytes, 3=8 bytes
mm = address mode:
    0+R=register, 4+R=register indirect, 8+R=offset,
    C/D = immediate value/address absolute
        Since mode 3 does not require a register, the register bits can be used to further modify the address mode.
    C = immediate
    D = address absolute – 32 bit address
ss = source register nbr: 0...3
dd = destination register nbr: 0...3

0-3 . x . y . z – Double Operand Integer

00nn xxxx mmss mmdd

xxxx = instruction

0 = add	8 = divu
1 = add with SP replacing R3	9 = div
2 = and	A = mulu
3 = ashift	B = mul
4 = bitest	C = or
5 = compare	D = sub
6 = copy	E = xor
7 = copy with SP replacing R3	F =

4-7 . 8 . y . z – Single Operand Integer

01nn 1000 yyyy mm(dd/ss)

immediate mode not practical except for push

yyyy = instruction

0 = addc
1 = clear
2 = com = 2s complement
3 = decrement pointer (decrement by operand size)
4 = decrement
5 = increment pointer (increment by operand size)
6 = increment
7 = inv = 1s complement
8 = pop
9 = subc
A = swap – swap bytes: nn=1: 0<–>1, nn=2: 0,1<–>2,3,
nn=3: 0...3<–>4...7
B = sxt – sign extend
C = test
D = psrcopy – does not use operand size (nn=0)
E =
F = push

4-7 . 9 . y . z – Rotate and Shift

01nn 1001 yyyy mmdd

yyyy = instruction

0 = rl rotate left	8 = sla shift left arithmetic
1 = rlc rotate left w/Carry	9 = sll shift left logical
2 = rr rotate right	A = sllc shift left logical w/Carry
3 = rrc rotate right w/Carry	B = sra shift right arithmetic
4 = rlb rotate left byte	C = srl shift right logical

5 = rrb rotate right byte	D = srlc shift right logical w/Carry
6 =	E =
7 =	F =

4-7 . A . y . z – Floating Point

01nn 1010 xyyy 00rr Floating Point operations: R0=destination

nn = valid only for opcodes 0 and 1

x = 0 = Single Precision, x = 1 = Double Precision

yyy = instruction

- 0 = FP to integer
- 1 = integer to FP
- 2 = FP add
- 3 = FP sub
- 4 = FP multiply
- 5 = FP divide
- 6 = to SP/DP
- 7 = compare

4-7 . B . y . z – Register Set

01nn 1011 yyyy zzzz

zzzz = register set or mask

yyyy = instruction

0 = rsdef	– set default register set <zzzz>
1 = rscopy	– copy current register set to register set <zzzz>
2 = rsexch	– exchange current register set with register set <zzzz>
3 = pushr	– register mask (R0, R1, R2, R3) = <zzzz>
4 = popr	– register mask (R3, R2, R1, R0) = <zzzz>
5 = setipl	– set the interrupt priority level = <zzz>
6 =	
7 =	
8..B rexch	– exchange a register with the same one in another RS, reg nbr in __yy, RS in zzzz
C..F rcopy	– copy a register to the same one in another RS, reg nbr in __yy, RS in zzzz

4-7 . C . 0-4 . z – Short I/O (the word following the instruction is the 16 bit I/O address)

01nn 1100 0000 mmss	copy the source to the I/O register
01nn 1100 0001 mmdd	copy the I/O register to the destination
01nn 1100 0010 mmss	logical-or the source with the I/O register as the destination
01nn 1100 0011 mmss	logical-and the source with the I/O register as the destination
01nn 1100 0100 nnnn	test a specific bit (nnnn: 0=15) in the I/O register, only Z bit is affected

4-7 . C . 8 . 0-2 – Block Copy

block copy: R0=count, R1=source address, R2=destination address
R0 is decremented until it reaches 0 as the data is copied; the instructions can be interrupted.

01nn 1100 1000 0000	R1 and R2 are incremented
01nn 1100 1000 0001	same as block copy except only R2 is not incremented. This is useful for writing a block of data to an I/O port.
01nn 1011 1000 0010	same as block copy except R1 is not incremented. This is useful for reading a block of data from an I/O port.

4 . C . 8 . 8-F – Condition Code

0100 1100 1000 10zz	clear condition code zz (0=N, 1=Z, 2=C, 3=V)
0100 1100 1000 11zz	set condition code zz

4 . D . y . z – Jump/Call

bit 7: 0 = jmp,	1 = call
bit 6: 0 = address,	1 = register
bit 5: 0 = absolute,	1 = relative
bit 4: 0 = long address,	1 = short address

0100 1101 0000 0000	jump to the 32 bit address following the instruction
0100 1101 1000 0000	call the function at the 32 bit address following the instruction

0100 1101 0001 zzzz	jump absolute using zzzz + next word as address
0100 1101 1001 zzzz	call absolute using zzzz + next word as address
0100 1101 0011 zzzz	jump relative using zzzz + next word as offset
0100 1101 1011 zzzz	call relative using zzzz + next word as offset
0100 1101 0100 00rr	jump to the address in the register
0100 1101 1100 00rr	call the function at the address in the register
0100 1101 0110 00rr	jump relative to the offset in the register
0100 1101 1110 00rr	call relative to the offset in the register
0100 1101 1111 0001	return from subroutine
0100 1101 1111 0010	return from interrupt
0100 1101 1111 0011	wait for interrupt

8-9 . x . yz – Decrement and Branch

yz = offset/2 (allows branches of approx +/- 512 Bytes)

1000 00rr oooo oooo	DBNE
1001 00rr oooo oooo	DBGE

A . x . yz – Branch

1010 xxxx oooo oooo

yz = offset/2 (allows branches of approx +/- 512 Bytes)

xxxx = branch condition code

0 = BR (unconditional)		8 = BVC	
1 = BCS		9 = BGE	(N = V)
2 = BCC		A = BLT	(N != V)
3 = BEQ	(BZS)	B = BGT	(Z = 0 & N = V)
4 = BNE	(BZC)	C = BLE	(Z = 1 | N != V)
5 = BMI	(BNS)	D = BGTU	(C = 1 & Z = 0)
6 = BPL	(BNC)	E = BLEU	(C = 0 | Z = 1)
7 = BVS		F =	

Index